The Long-life Heart

How to Avoid Heart Disease and Live
a Longer Life

DR ARABELLA MELVILLE and
COLIN JOHNSON

CENTURY ARROW

London Melbourne Auckland Johannesburg

For Pru, Jay and Fran, for the qualities of their hearts.

For the memory of Leonard Rossiter, who filled our hearts with pleasure.

A Century Arrow Book
Published by Arrow Books Limited
62-65 Chandos Place, London WC2N 4NW

An imprint of Century Hutchinson Ltd

London Melbourne Sydney Auckland Johannesburg
and agencies throughout the world

First published by Century 1985
Century Arrow edition 1986

Printed and bound in Great Britain by
The Guernsey Press Co. Ltd
Guernsey, Channel Islands

ISBN 0 09 946660 0

Contents

Acknowledgements

We would like to thank Dr Peter Nixon for reading and commenting on our manuscript, for his generosity with information, and his many helpful suggestions.

We are indebted to Sarah Riddell for her sure and certain editorial touch.

Our thanks are also due to the British Heart Foundation, and the staff of the Health Education Council library.

Lastly we must acknowledge our gratitude to our colleagues at Life Profile Ltd who have allowed us to disrupt their work and who helped in the preparation of this book.

Notes on Terminology

Plain English is not often used to describe heart disease and things associated with the problem. Although many medical terms, such as 'coronary', have slipped into common use with the increase in the disease, they are not always understood.

We have tried to avoid jargon and medical terminology, but at times it is not possible. Below are terms which appear in the text, with a brief explanation of their meaning. This explanation is not intended to be academically exhaustive, but to help general readers in their understanding of the heart disease problem.

First, we have used the term 'heart disease' to cover all degenerative conditions associated with the heart and circulatory system. These range from a heart attack, through hardening of the arteries and the bursting of blood vessels (strokes) to problems caused by poor circulation. The context in which the term heart disease is used should make its precise meaning clear.

Angina: Chest pain caused by an overtaxed heart.

Artery: A major blood vessel which carries blood from the heart to other parts of the body.

Arteriosclerosis: Hardening of the arteries. This is usually associated with atheroma.

Atheroma: A deposit of fatty material in the lining of arteries. Atheroma can become so severe that major vessels are clogged.

Blood pressure: The pressure at which the blood is pumped through major arteries. Blood pressure fluctuates according to health and anticipated need.

Bradycardia: Slow heart-rate.

Cardiac: Of, or relating to, the heart.

Cardiologist: A medical practitioner who specialises in treating heart disease.

Cardiovascular: Of the heart and blood vessels.

Cerebral: Of the brain.

Cholesterol: A fat-like substance found in animal tissue; the main component of atheroma.

Claudication: Limping. See *Intermittent claudication*, below.

Coronary arteries: Major arteries which provide a blood supply for the heart itself.

Coronary heart disease: Illness associated with atheroma in the coronary arteries.

Coronary spasm: Contraction of the coronary arteries which results in a drastic reduction in blood supply to the heart. This is a common cause of angina.

Diabetes: A condition in which blood sugar levels tend to be abnormally high. If diabetes is uncontrolled, sugar spills into the urine.

Embolism: Blockage of an artery by a blood clot or air bubble. It is most often associated with atheroma.

Epidemiology: The study of the pattern of disease in populations.

Haemoglobin: The pigment in the red cells of the blood which acts as a carrier for oxygen and carbon dioxide. Haemoglobin is a complex protein which includes iron.

Haemorrhage: Bleeding, usually severe or otherwise clinically important.

Heart attack: Myocardial infarction (see below).

Heart failure: A condition in which the heart cannot pump sufficiently strongly to meet the needs of the body. It causes accumulation of fluid in the body (*oedema*)

Hormone: A substance released by the body to control the function of particular parts.

Hypercholesterolaemia: Unusually high levels of cholesterol in the blood stream.

Hypertension: Unusually high blood pressure, maintained consistently over a period of months or more.

Hyperuricaemia: High levels of uric acid (a normal product of cell breakdown) in the blood. The main symptom is gout, a painful inflammation of a joint – often in the big toe.

Intermittent claudication: Pain in the legs, usually the calves, with exercise. It is caused by inadequate blood supply to working muscles.

Ischaemia: Inadequate blood supply. Ischaemic heart disease refers to inadequate flow of blood through the coronary arteries to feed the heart. This may be due to coronary spasm or blockage, or both.

Myocardial infarction: Heart attack. Part of the heart muscle dies because an inadequate blood supply brings insufficient oxygen (see *Ischaemia*, above). The disturbance of heart rhythm which often results means that the heart no longer pumps effectively.

Oedema: Fluid retention in the body tissues. It can result from heart failure, which results in back-pressure in the veins, and kidney disease.

Sphygmomanometer: A device used to measure blood pressure.

Tachycardia: Fast heart-rate.

Thrombosis: Formation of a blood clot inside a blood vessel or in the heart.

Vein: A vessel which carries blood from the body to the heart.

Foreword

A century ago, exhaustion was an important medical topic. Its effects upon coping, endurance, resistance to illness, morale and performance were well understood. If exhaustion was not relieved, the heart would lose its ability to go on supporting effort. It would lose its competence through a range of mechanisms, varyin from purely functional disorders at one extreme to organic disease at the other. If the functional disorders were uppermost, the regulation of the heart rate and rhythm became unstable, the blood pressure rose extravagantly, and disordered breathing, nowadays called 'hyperventilation', caused chest pain, giddiness, sweating, aching and cramps in the limbs and back, and disordered function throughout the body. The illness caused by the impact of these disorders upon the daily life was called 'soldier's heart' or 'effort syndrome'. The heart that was long 'overtaxed by constant emotional influences or excessive physical activity, and thus deprived of its appropriate rest' became diseased. Narrowing of the coronary arteries and ischaemic damage of the heart muscle would be found. The illness caused by the impact of this disease on daily life was called angina pectoris, a diagnosis nowadays subdivided into effort angina, acute coronary insufficiency, myocardial infarction, and sudden coronary death. The amount of disease required to produce the illness was known to be variable. Some people had a great deal of disease but no symptoms. Others had severe disability but little disease. Patients with angina pectoris presented the same range of coronary arterial appearances as contemporaries without disability. Some recovered by natural means but others did not. It was clear that factors outside the coronary arterial system governed the impact of his disease on the patient's life, and exhaustion was the most important. If the patient could not become unexhausted he could not get well.

The Victorians saw close relationships between the functional disorders and the organic. They were aware that coronary arterial spasm might damage the lining of the artery and cause changes which led to the deposition of blood clot and the formation of rigid atheromatous plaque.

In this century there has been a huge advance in technology. The conversion of blood clot to atheromatous plaque has been demonstrated. Coronary arterial spasm has been studied by heart catheterisation, and it is now accepted that it can be triggered by hyperventilation. It is accepted that the severity of anginal pain bears almost no relationship to the extent of the disease in the coronary arteries. These days we understand that the ability of the body's self-regulating mechanisms (homoeostasis) to deal with the effects of effort is finite, and may be outstripped by the demands of a brain that imposes constant emotional influences and excessive physical effort, and rejects the need for appropriate rest. Wear and tear outstrip repair or, in today's jargon, the arousal of the brain mobilises all the mechanisms that produce energy for coping (catabolism) at the expense of the mechanisms for repair, maintenance and defence (anabolism). When catabolism has the upper hand it is common to find increased blood pressure, raised blood sugar, cholesterol and triglyceride levels, and a tendency to thrombosis. There is a rapid loss of fitness and very often a tendency to obesity and fluid retention. The subjects like cigarettes because the smoking helps them to concentrate and keep going in hard circumstances, and reduces feelings of aggression and frustration. These products of catabolism provide the greatest danger to the heart and arteries.

From my point of view the modern investigations confirm the commonsense of the cardiological tradition, but for those unaware of the tradition the picture is not so clear. Evangelism has distorted it since the 1939–45 War. Patients have wanted magic-bullet cures. The majority have not sought informed autonomy nor responsibility for the health of the bodies they inhabit. Some epidemiologists have sought to manipulate governments and the media, and even promise to rid us of the plague of heart disease if we follow their advice on risk factors. Unfortunately, these epidemiologists have been concerned with minor matters that can be counted, and not the major, uncountable factors that determine survival: mothering, early education, poverty and affluence, security, fitting in, social assets, control of one's life, coping, motivation, environmental stability, isolation, marriage and loss of spouse, for example.

The pharmaceutical industries have done well out of betablockers and other drugs for suppressing the symptoms of an overtaxed heart or modifying the catabolic products of overstretched homoeostasis, but doctors have got out of the habit of prescribing adequate conditions for anabolism and teaching patients to outwit the influences that cause exhaustion and angina. Patients continue to tax their hearts in self-defeating and damaging ways; consequently there is a high demand for surgical treatment by coronary artery bypass grafting. The operation may bypass some of the debris from the past and buy time for changing a way of life, but it is not a cure, and may not extend life except in those who belong to a small and favourable group. Many rehabilitation programmes teach patients how to take physical exercise, but neglect to train them for coping with the everyday activities and tensions of their lives.

The picture changed again in 1983. Protests against the post-war drift erupted in a startling fashion. The Medical Defence Union reported that litigation had become a growth industry. The media attacked conventional medicine and said much in support of the alternatives. The College of Health and Action for Victims of Medical Accidents were set up, and the foundations laid for the Institute of Complementary Medicine and the Council for Alternative and Complementary Medicine. The Journal of Alternative Medicine went into print. Conventional medicine had long been aware of George Engel's argument that its models of disease were no longer adequate for the scientific tasks and social responsibilities of the profession, and changes came from within. The British Holistic Medical Association, the International Society for Humanism in Cardiology and the Research Council for Complementary Medicine were created. British nurses accepted the Nursing Process, a change from a task-orientated to a patient-orientated role. In the U.S.A., an important medical school described a new system of education for humanism in medicine, and the Board of Internal Medicine announced it would seek humanistic qualities in applicants for its licence. The Church of England created a Ministry for Health and Healing. H.R.H. Prince Charles put his finger on the point when he said 'by concentrating on smaller and smaller fragments of the body, modern medicine loses sight of the patient as a whole being, and by reducing health to mechanical functioning it is no longer able to deal with the phenomenon of healing'. 'Healing' means to become whole or sound, to recover from a sickness or wound, to get well.

The essential works of healing and the processes of repair are provided by the body, and one of the first responsibilities of medicine is to provide the best possible conditions for the most effective deployment of the body's healing and repair systems (anabolism). In the Victorian era, Florence Nightingale and the leading heart specialists understood these conditions very well. Where possible, they followed Hippocrates' practice. The patient was allowed to sleep and rest until he recovered from his exhaustion, and provided with an enjoyable period of convalescence. When he was ready, the physician who had 'entered into his life' and learned about the problems which caused the exhaustion helped him to make the best of himself and fight back. In angina it was particularly important to avoid pain, to obtain adequate sleep ('it is axiomatic that the patient will not get well without it'), to temper emotional arousal, to keep a fitting balance between rest and effort, and to boost morale. The Established Church contributed tactics for relaxing and calming the breathing (*vide* Gregory of Sinai's 'Prayer of the Heart').

It appears to me that patients still need these traditional or basic services, well employed and integrated sensibly with the best of modern technology. They are not difficult to find in the N.H.S. if the physician supports the nurses' ability to provide adequate sleep and rest, and makes full use of the occupational therapists' ability to teach the patient how to cope with the activities and tensions of everyday life. A wider variety of services for prevention is available outside the N.H.S.

Teaching and counselling are an essential part of the therapeutic approach because the patient is not naturally equipped for dealing with a heart that refuses to make the effort demanded of it. Incapable of quitting his duties and obligations, and blind to the needs of his body, he is likely to work up a catabolic system of arousal that can destroy him. He must be led into safety and taught how to fight in a better way.

Melville and Johnson have done well to keep their feet when the subject of their book is swaying so strongly. They have straddled the pre- and post-1983 swings of fashion and incorporated them with much of the traditional basic care. Their writing is punctuated with marvellous flashes of insight, and is well worth reading simply for the truth that the exhausted person is not in a position to see and deal with the causes of his own exhaustion. The authors are well aware that the circumstances which cause the heart to hurt must be avoided or outwitted. Their model of the ship is extremely well chosen for its clarification of the issues involved in manoeuvring oneself out of a course of ill-health.

Do they succeed in their claim to have prescribed methods for avoiding heart disease and living a longer life? It would be impossible to mount a trial to prove their case scientifically and, in the absence of such proof, I would give them the contemporary prize for making the best effort.

Peter Nixon

Consultant Cardiologist, Charing Cross Hospital (London)

Founder Member of the International Society for Humanism in Cardiology

Introduction

Heart and circulatory diseases have become the most common cause of death in the world. Human beings are suffering an epidemic of diseases which affect their most vital bodily organ and its associated systems. Not only is this epidemic claiming more victims decade by decade, but the age of the victims is decreasing. What used to be considered degenerative conditions of old age have progressively moved to claim younger groups of the population. Even those in their early teens often show the preliminary signs of degeneration that are associated with heart and circulatory disease. This move down the age range has gone so far that some specialists now consider heart disease to be a paediatric problem.

The avoidance of heart disease is a complex question. Untold millions spent on research, countless years of medical practice aimed at cure, the application of sophisticated technology and the exploration of a myriad of alternative therapies have not held it in check.

A vast amount of detailed research into the bodily functions involved has been carried out. Some useful indicators have emerged pointing to causes and many key features of the development of the conditions have been identified. And yet, almost in spite of each new discovery, more questions are raised than are answered. If the results of research into heart disease are typified by one quality, it is contradiction.

The conclusion that one is forced towards is that there is no one simple answer to heart disease. If there were, it would surely have been found by now. Indeed, the very opposite may be nearer the truth: there are many answers and individuals have to find their own personal routes to survival.

Heart disease, in all its manifestations, has a multi-causal network. While it is possible to spell out general factors which will adversely affect many people and recommend that they be avoided, conscientious avoidance of every known predisposing factor would surely make life impossible. The contradictions of the heart disease problem which confront us at the practical level are obvious. We all know people who break all the accepted rules and remain rudely healthy, as well as joggers and fitness fans who suffer fatal heart attacks.

To resolve the apparent contradictions and plot our individual paths to a long heart life, we have to take a step back and make a cool reappraisal of ourselves and the behaviour of our species. At the root of the complex nature of heart disease is the very complexity of our own natures; this complexity is frequently confounded by the simplistic approach we adopt to many things.

Although complex and diverse, we have become a successful species because we are supreme generalists. We do not need highly specialised diet, habitat or climate. We can tolerate a wider range of all these things than any other large mammal, and those that we cannot conquer naturally we modify with technology to suit our needs. Yet despite our success, we have created for ourselves many problems. We all share an uneasiness about the direction we are taking. This uneasiness has led many thinkers to begin a basic reassessment of our species and its place in the scheme of things. For most of us the philosophical question of 'What are we?' gives way to the more practical question of 'Should we live in this way?'

Heart disease (together with cancers and a variety of other metabolic disorders) has been dubbed a 'disease of civilisation'. This is because it only assumes epidemic proportions under the conditions in which modern Western industrialised populations live. In attempting to refine this definition to establish a cause, some people have tried to pin the blame exclusively on an ill-defined 'lifestyle' which allows the disease to proliferate.

Considerations of how we live may not be the whole answer

because our lifestyle is not a product of 'civilisation', but of our Western industrialised culture. It is in the matrix of this culture that some of the final answers to the heart disease conundrum will have to be found. This is not to imply that smoking and the other classical contributory factors are not relevant, or that lifestyle is not important, but they account for only a small part of the total picture. The structure of your life within your culture may also damage heart health in ways which should not be ignored. Obsessive attention to a limited group of simplistic risk factors is not the answer.

The causes of heart disease seem shifting and elusive, difficult to pin down and consequently difficult for the individual to deal with. To increase your heart life you need to adopt positive measures which match the scope and adaptability of the disease you are fighting.

To make the situation more understandable we need a vision of the process of the disease which moves away from ideas of simple causes having simple effects. This does not solve the question of heart disease. Even combining simple causes and relating them to a variety of effects does not work. What we need to develop is a multi-dimensional image.

The illustration that seems most suitable is that of a passenger taking a journey on a ship. Passengers can make many choices about details of their voyage; how to spend time, which deck, bars and restaurants to use, when to sleep and so on. There will, however, be limitations; the food you want may not be on board, or you might not be able to find or afford it; you will not be welcome in the engine room or crew quarters. Ultimately you are confined to the ship itself.

There is much that individual passengers have control over, but beyond this they must fit in with what is provided, applicable or imposed on them. Most important in day-to-day terms will be the way the ship is run. While in theory this may be open to discussion or representation and change, in practice things will have been done in a certain way for a long time, everyone is used to it, and changing details will possibly have so many unforeseeable repercussions that there will be resistance even to the idea of change. And if individuals decide to change their personal routine, it will be at a cost; if you decide to sleep all day and stay up all night, getting food might be difficult because the people who provide the food will not want to change their routine. And you will all be constrained by the physical nature of the ship, whether you are on a luxury liner or an old tramp. It will be so long and so wide, your accommodation will be fixed and have certain facilities. Within the ship passengers and crew must interact to complete the voyage. It will be easier to conform to the social conventions provided by the dynamics of life on board.

Our ship is based on high technology. With its engines and air conditioning, its sophisticated navigational equipment and its stabilised furnished environment, it can create the illusion that wind, weather and ocean currents no longer affect us. Yet it is an illusion. All the elemental forces that have influenced past voyages are still operating in the outside world.

Today we may have deeper understanding of some of these forces, such as the weather. Some we will have modified or overcome, such as the effects of tides and currents near harbours. But there are others of which we are only now becoming aware; how they affect our voyage is not certain. What is certain is that it would be unwise to discount them simply because we are unaware of their precise effects.

So how does our picture work in relation to avoiding heart disease? The way passengers behave will influence the way in which the voyage affects them, as do the choices we exercise in our daily lives. The ship contains its passengers and crew much as our society and culture contain us. And just as the ship is moved by winds and currents, so our culture is influenced by movements and events within wider human society. All of these forces reach us, as surely as the wind and waves reach us on board ship.

On land and at sea, one of the most tangible divisions in society has always been between the haves and the have-nots.

Just as important is the division now between the knows and the know-nots.

Those who know what is happening to them and the world in which they live have a better chance of surviving and thriving. Those who know and care need not be victims of the forces generated within our culture which produce heart disease. If enough of us become knows, of course, the culture itself will change. For all long-term questions of health and well-being this is the only realistic final objective.

At this point, before considering in detail the practical aspects of heart health, we want to offer a glimpse of the point to which our intellectual journey leads. The crucial question which we must answer is this: what is it about our Western industrial culture that makes so many of us into victims of heart disease?

Any definition of what it is that brings about heart disease must have sufficient breadth to encapsulate all the phenomena that characterise the problem. It must, therefore, tend towards the philosophical rather than the medical, towards theory rather than practice. However, such a definition is essential to our efforts to understand and avoid heart disease, and from it practical implications can be derived.

Our conclusion is that heart disease is the result of the disruption of anticipation.

Disruption can happen at all levels of our existence. Its essence is that a sequence of events is not completed in the way that was anticipated. As a crude example, if you put water in your car's petrol tank, everything will function as before, the pipes, filters and pump will get the water to the carburettor, the gauge will even tell you how much there is in your tank; the carburettor will mix the water with air, but the motor will not run. The anticipation of the total system breaks down because although water does everything else, it does not burn like petrol.

Although our bodies are not as simple or as mechanical as cars, all their systems have anticipatory sequences. When we put something in our mouths and swallow it, we have a complex digestive system ready and waiting, and anticipating that it will be food. It reacts to the prospect of food before anything goes into the mouth. All our systems have anticipation built in. For instance, the balance organs in our ears assume that we will be standing on the fixed and stable surface of the earth. The constant movement of waves under our feet disrupts this system, and we end up feeling sea-sick.

The sort of disruption that causes heart disease can vary from the discontinuity of a metabolic process at the molecular level, right up to the complex emotional upheaval caused by loss of a loved one or the fruits of a lifetime's work. Disruption causes inappropriate reactions which may vary from the deposition of cholesterol in arteries to faulty heart rhythms and the bursting of blood vessels.

Many of us have complicated the picture by teaching our systems to anticipate things which are in themselves harmful. Nicotine from cigarettes is the obvious example. When we correct harmful habits, we have to confront the problem of disruption of our adaptation to the original disruption.

The common denominator linking different types of disruption of anticipation is the interpretation of information. To avoid disruption we need to supply the right information to our minds and bodies, whether in the form of the right molecules or proportions of food, or in the right nervous system stimulation. What is right for us is whatever our systems have evolved to expect.

We can use our intelligence to alter our perception and behaviour so that our anticipation is correct at many levels of life. But we have to recognise that there are other, immutable parts of our nature. When we have sorted out which are which, and adjusted accordingly, then we shall be on our way to ending the heart disease epidemic.

The immediate purpose of this book is to enable you to find yourself in relation to heart disease: to assess your risk at various levels and to map out positive measures that will enable you to improve measurably your chances of avoiding it. Our picture of a passenger on a ship will indicate the several levels at which you have to approach this task. You need to equip yourself with knowledge relevant to your journey, then make sure that you are on the right ship, with suitable facilities, and sailing in the right direction. Each of us can journey through life without premature death or disability. It is a matter of finding what is right and important for us.

At the end you should be a wiser traveller, equipped with the ground rules for increasing your heart life and living a longer and happier life, perhaps with the broadened mind that travel is supposed to confer. We hope that your voyage through this book is enjoyable and that your journey through life is enhanced.

Bon voyage!

Colin Johnson and Arabella Melville
Beccles, Suffolk,
November 1984

CHAPTER 1

The Problem

The web of life is of a mingled yarn,
good and ill together

William Shakespeare *All's Well That Ends Well*

The flat tyre stopped Dave short as he was about to jump into his car. He cursed the rain, cursed his next appointment, and cursed the fact that he had bothered to stop for lunch. As he wrestled with the jack, waves of indigestion came over him. An old problem. The last thing he did was curse the garage gorilla who had tightened his wheel nuts. Pain like a sledgehammer blow dropped Dave to the wet ground. He was dead on arrival at hospital.

Dave had become, in a matter of minutes, another statistic in the heart disease epidemic. He had died in that most unacceptable way, a victim of the heart attack that strikes apparently out of the blue, prematurely killing the father of a young family in his prime. This is a phenomenon of our times, a once-rare occurrence that has increased dramatically in prevalence over the past fifty years.

Today heart disease is the world's leading cause of death. It accounts for half of all deaths in affluent countries, and for more than one death in three worldwide. Year by year, as the problem spreads, communities and groups which once enjoyed relative freedom from this modern scourge see more of their members succumb to it.

Dave had his fatal heart attack at the age of thirty-eight. It was a possibility that simply had not occurred to him or to his young widow Carole. Her grief constantly threatened to overwhelm her as she struggled to rear their four young sons. A suddenly much reduced income added to her burden.

How tragic that their lives should collapse in this way, when Dave had been working so hard to secure a perfect future for his family! Six months before, they had moved from their West Country home to what was to be their dream cottage by a rushing Welsh stream. Dave, an ambitious sales represent-ative, had launched into a new phase of his career, opening up the Welsh market for his company's products. He expected an income that would rise steadily in return for a determined effort in the early stages. It was just a matter of one big sustained push.

He knew, of course, that he was asking a lot of himself, but he was a confident individual. Having committed himself, he could not afford to take days off. Part of their dream was the house; it needed extensive renovation, so Dave could not relax at week-ends or in the evening. The twins, scarcely a year old, made it all even more difficult. Night after night they woke, screaming in unison; and while Carole coped well, Dave needed every hour of sleep he could get. But he overrode his weariness, rising early every morning, however disturbed the night had been.

The tiredness he felt in those last weeks did not alert him to any danger. He thought it was only to be expected. He never had had cause for anxiety about his health, he rarely even caught colds, and hadn't seen a doctor in years. Anyway, there were no definite symptoms; he was able to continue working; and he coped by drinking a little more coffee, smoking a few more cigarettes. It wouldn't go on for ever.

Perhaps he attributed the increasing indigestion to hurried meals, for he could not afford the time to linger; perhaps to too much coffee. He sucked antacid tablets, drove on and dismissed the recurring annoyance. It is, after all, common enough. With his commitments pushing him and his dream before him, nothing would stop Dave working.

From the time the attack began to Dave's death was a matter of minutes. He collapsed, struggling for breath and clutching at his chest. In seconds he lost consciousness. A passing stranger, seeing him turn blue on the ground, ran to call a doctor. An ambulance was called immediately, but there was nothing to be done: it was already too late.

Dave was one of the twenty-five per cent of men who have their first heart attack between the ages of thirty-five and sixty. When a young man is struck down unexpectedly, the chances that he will die suddenly are higher than for someone older, but overall, more than half survive. In the period following the first heart attack, the risk of a second remains high; it might come within days, months, or years. Yet those who take it as a final warning that they must change their way of living may achieve greater resilience as a result.

About one person in five with heart disease does not have that choice. The first clear symptom is also the last: sudden death. Between 1950 and 1970, the proportion of men of thirty-four to fifty-four years old who died from heart attacks doubled. By 1983, one death in three in men of this age was due to heart attack.

How sudden is sudden death? Certainly, to those who do not understand potential health problems, it may be totally unexpected. But for most people there are warning signs; few victims are completely unaware of failing health during the build-up period.

Performance starts to deteriorate, and the person finds insufficient energy to meet normal demands, for as much as a year before the final blow. Often widows of heart attack victims will recall that their husbands started falling asleep in their chairs, even during meals; how they gave up favourite activities one after another, complaining they had not the energy or had lost interest in them; and how they gradually ceased to be able to do things that held little challenge even months before.

Unfortunately, those who do not notice something amiss tend not to take appropriate action to avert the risk; either they do not realise the seriousness of the situation or they are not aware of the actions they must take.

Nor do most doctors recognise the build-up to sudden death. Even if they could assess the degree of damage to the crucial blood vessels which feed the heart, doctors would be unlikely to discover signs of imminent death; for the system often seems, at post-mortem, too healthy to fail. Death comes despite relatively mild disease and little damage to the coronary arteries.

Most of us in Western countries are familiar with heart and blood vessel disease. We may accept it, as far as we can accept any sort of disease, any cause of death. We assure ourselves that the old must die of something, and reserve our dread for that second fearsome killer of our society, cancer. We forget how many more lives are destroyed or foreshortened by lingering damage to the blood circulatory system.

At least half of all heart attack victims have had unambiguous warnings. They realise that sudden exertion, the effort of clearing snow or pushing a car, an emotional crisis, a heated argument, a heavy meal, or any serious threat to their personal equilibrium could be too much. Many heart patients also know when their systems are failing to meet their needs. They experience the deficit as angina. This is typically a pain in the chest of crushing intensity, brought on by physical effort or by anything which causes the heart to pump faster: even anticipation of a stressful event may be enough to bring on angina.

Gregory has lived with angina for two years. Maybe it will go on for another ten years; or maybe next week, next month, the angina attack won't end when he stops and takes his nitroglycerin, but shade into the unremitting pain that heralds a full-blown heart attack. The fear he understandably feels when angina starts makes the problem worse, but he controls it as best he can. Familiarity is reducing the sense of threat.

But his life is strictly limited by his condition. Gregory runs a small shop, and now has to be extremely careful. He must remember not to walk too fast, not to get into arguments with staff or suppliers and to avoid situations that will irritate him. Life has become a hazardous minefield where any wrong move will trigger pain. Yet he knows that if only he could take it easy he might stand a chance. It might even be possible to get rid of the condition and become his old healthy self. But there is the shop, and his responsibilities; he feels he is caught in a trap with no obvious way out.

His doctor put him on tablets. They help to control his condition, but they will not cure it. They keep attacks at bay by making him calmer, soothing the heart, as his doctor explained. Without them, he would find it virtually impossible to carry on the business. But they have their drawbacks: cold hands and feet, dizziness when he gets up, a general feeling of flatness. One of the worst aspects of the whole sorry business is the damage to his married life. Gregory tries not to think about that; the total disappearance of his sex life, not surprisingly, upsets him. He has to try to keep calm nowadays, and trust his wife to understand.

Angina has become very common in Britain. It is the first clear symptom of disease in a quarter of heart patients, though angina itself is usually preceded by periods of chronic tiredness. It may precede or follow a heart attack. In one sense it can be a boon, for it warns the sufferer of the risk he or she runs, and the pain demands that strain on the heart be reduced to less dangerous levels. But it is nevertheless associated with early death from heart attack.

Among men over the age of forty, and women over fifty-five, the incidence of angina in some communities can rise to afflict as many as one person in four. This was the prevalence of angina detected among women of the Rhondda Valley in south Wales. Other research has shown that angina is about equally common in men and women, although men are considerably more likely to suffer heart attacks after a period of angina. Male angina victims run four times the risk of death from heart disease within five years, when compared with those who are free from angina.

In general practice, doctors see patients with angina about as often as they are called to attend cases of acute heart attack. Between them, these two types of related event account for nine out of ten new cases of heart disease. Only one person in five is likely to avoid death or serious disablement in the five years from the time the first symptom was brought to a doctor's attention, for the disease is usually far advanced already when these symptoms develop.

Angina is caused by constriction of the coronary arteries, the blood vessels which supply the blood to the muscle of the heart. This constriction has two underlying mechanisms, atheroma and spasm. Perhaps because they are constantly in use these arteries seem particularly prone to damage, and angina usually emerges in susceptible people earlier in life than other similar conditions. But the development of atheroma and spasm also interferes with the blood supply to other muscles, with similar if not so potentially lethal results. Pain in the legs is the usual warning that muscles are being deprived of oxygen. The symptoms range from occasional cramps to sharp pain, and can eventually reach the point where gangrene sets in.

Mike is an ex-miner who knows he must lose part of each leg. His diseased arteries are now inadequate to deliver sufficient blood to keep his feet alive. Amputation is the only solution. The problem has gone too far for any other remedy. Without surgery the rot that has already started in his flesh will spread. Amputation is an unpleasant prospect, but Mike will not miss his feet now; the pain stopped him walking some time ago. The progression was insidious, beginning with a tendency to cold, blue feet. That was easily enough dealt with: he took to wearing woolly bedsocks and invested in an electric blanket. He viewed it as one of those predictable signs of increasing age and did not worry too much.

Next he suffered cramping pains in the calves. These became a nightly annoyance and were dealt with in a similar manner to the cold. Mike found that if he hung the uncomfortable limb out of the bed, the cramps were usually reduced to the point where he could sleep. His legs were looking progressively more unpleasant as time went on, but he ignored that too. He was past sixty – too old for vanity, he told himself. Pain in his calves limited the distance he could walk. Before long, even a slight hill became too much to tackle without frequent rests to allow the cramp to subside. The once strong coal-face worker took to using a stick. That way he could still be sufficiently mobile to get his groceries in the day and reach the pub in the evening.

It was when a small injury turned into an unpleasant ulcer which refused to heal that Mike realised he did need help. His doctor dressed the ulcer, gave him a prescription for his circulation, and told him to give up smoking; but after forty years on thirty a day, it wasn't that easy. Much too late the doctor advised him to walk more. He could not when the pain would come on so quickly and so regularly. Besides, he never had been much of a walker: the miles underground had been quite enough. The surgeon's assessment of the situation was grim. The artery feeding the leg was constricted and furred up over most of its length. Mike would have to lose part of each leg and both feet. In the hospital ward Mike found he was not alone. Half of those there had the same problem as him; their legs were being pruned, as it were. Mike envied those who had wives to look after them. His fiercely guarded independence was over. He felt there would be little to live for now that he was so disabled.

Mike and his middle-aged or elderly companions in the male surgical ward were all fairly heavy smokers. Everybody has known for years that smoking causes lung cancer, but only recently has it been realised that it also damages the major blood vessels. It seems to cause constrictions like kinks in a pipe. Combined with an unsuitable diet and lack of suitable exercise, over the years trouble accumulates.

All of the cases we have so far considered are typical of those who contribute to the total of 300,000 people who die in Britain each year from heart and circulatory disease. Most of these deaths are premature and avoidable. Heart and circulatory diseases account for more deaths in Britain than any other cause – killing twice as many people as all cancers, and 14 times more than injuries and poisonings. Heart disease is also Britain's most expensive illness. Over 62 million working days are lost every year to industry and commerce as a result of diseases of the heart and circulation.

One area of the problem where there has been intense medical activity is that of high blood pressure – hypertension. Doctors, aware that intervention to reduce the number of deaths must begin earlier, now treat people for high blood pressure even if they have no unpleasant symptoms. During the 1970s, there was a massive increase in the rate of diagnosis of this condition, and a parallel increase in the number of people who became dependent on an assortment of drugs aimed at reducing their blood pressure. The rationale for this is the well-documented association between high blood pressure and heart attacks, strokes, and kidney failure.

Janet had no symptoms at all when she consulted a doctor for a routine insurance check. She had been a bit tense, had had problems sleeping; but at that consultation she learnt that she could be risking heart disease or a stroke. Her blood vessels were being damaged by high blood pressure. When her own doctor confirmed this Janet, who thought of herself as a fit and able career girl, suddenly found she was transformed into a chronically sick, pill-taking patient. She had been told that she'd have to take drugs for the rest of her life if she was to minimise the prospect of premature death.

Janet now felt she was caught in a trap – one she bitterly resented. Her doctor had explained what could happen if she decided not to comply with his instructions. She remembers him telling her that the small blood vessels feeding her brain could fracture with the strain, just as any pipe will eventually burst when liquid is forced through it at excessive pressure. The heart would be suffering too, and the coronary vessels which feed it.

He also explained the classic vicious circle: high blood pressure damages the walls of the arteries, which in turn leads to a build-up of cholesterol deposits; these narrow the arteries, reducing the amount of blood that can get through. This not only leads to even higher blood pressure but also increases the danger of heart attack. Additionally the pressure against the heart valves weakens them; pressure in the kidneys interferes with their filtering efficiency; and the result could be the accumulation of fluid in the tissues. Eventually, her heart would fail.

Faced with this prospect, Janet, like millions of others, took the tablets. The warning for her was underlined by a younger woman she had interviewed as a journalist some months before. Clare had claimed that oral contraceptives had caused her brain haemorrhage.

Clare had woken in hospital to find that her right side did not function any more. With the dawning realisation came the horror that she, only just past thirty, could be crippled. Since that dreadful day when she had fallen unconscious in the kitchen, things had improved. When Janet interviewed Clare, her speech had been clear enough, but the two halves of her face didn't match. Janet found it disconcerting at first, watching the lop-sided mouth, the droopy eye that didn't move like its partner. Apparently, it had all improved very considerably over the year that had passed.

The reality proved to be less harsh than Clare had initially feared, though coping with her illness did demand all the emotional resources she could muster. Gradually the paralysed parts were coming to life again; first her leg, then her arm. Slowly her toes began to move and her muscles regained some of their strength. Finally she was learning to control her fingers again; but while she could now form her fingers into the shape required to pick up objects, she could not yet shift any weight. She continued to practise, determined that she would recover.

She detailed for Janet the effects of her illness on her life. 'For nine months I've had to wear shifts, I can't cope with fasteners. Everything becomes a problem when only one side works properly. You can't peel potatoes, open tins, get out of the bath or even cut up your own food. My husband had to do so many things for me.' Clare became depressed. 'You can imagine, all your closest friends start to fade away after a while, perhaps because you are always asking more than you can give. I got to be very embarrassed, having to ask for help all the time. Life seemed impossible. I couldn't see the point in getting up any more.'

When Janet met her she was bouncing back. 'I just thank God that I'm not worse affected, and that I am recovering the use of my right side. I've heard of women – one a girl of only seventeen – who are worse than I am. And how could I have managed if I'd had young children?'

Although strokes are still relatively uncommon among young women, their frequency has increased markedly over the past twenty years. And while the death-toll in 1983 for the twenty-five to forty-four years age-group was fairly low at 365, this figure reflects a much larger problem.

At least 5,000 women a year under the age of forty-five survive a stroke to face the possibility of a lifetime of disablement.

The individuals whose case histories we have considered represent the most easily identifiable types of heart disease sufferers. Although they account for hundreds of thousands of deaths, there are millions more who are hypertensives, and behind them are masses who suffer from a host of other related symptoms and problems. These are as diverse as types of blindness and kidney failure, and extend to what can only be described as premature senility. All are part of the heart disease problem.

Before considering wider aspects of the heart disease problem, we have to think a little about the actual parts of the body involved: the heart and its associated plumbing, the arteries and veins, and the fluid pumped through this system, the blood. This most vital of all our systems affects, and in its turn is affected by, every other part of the body. It is little wonder that, if something goes wrong, the symptoms can be so widespread.

We do not need the sort of detail of the system that is popular, particularly with colour illustrators, in medical and pseudo-medical textbooks. To have a healthy heart it is only necessary to understand why things happen; leave precisely how to the experts. Part of the wonder of the whole cardiovascular system is that it does so much without our being aware of it. And this is, of course, how it should be. If we lived in ways that promoted health, this book would not be necessary.

Every part of the body needs blood to survive. It carries the oxygen and glucose that provide the energy to support life, the proteins from which our cells are built and replaced, the hormones that control our complicated chemistry, the defence systems that fight infection. Blood removes waste products including cell debris and carbon dioxide. Short of blood, our cells die; some in seconds, others in minutes.

The role of the heart, obviously, is crucial. It is the pump that forces blood round the body. The rate varies from 5 to 30 litres a minute, according to need. A total pump failure means that the whole system fails at once. In a heart attack the failure is generally thought to be the consequence of inadequate blood supply to a part of the heart muscle itself. For the heart tissue needs blood to survive, and it is delivered by coronary arteries, so called because they encircle the heart like a crown.

Blood vessel disease is damage to the delivery system. It could be a sudden failure, blocked by a clot at a crucial point; or blood flow through the vessels may be chronically inadequate to meet more than minimal demands. Illness may develop fast, or it can be gradual, limiting life for years before the end finally comes. The cause may be cholesterol, clogging the arteries, but cholesterol alone rarely accounts for the severity of the problem. The arteries are also capable of contracting suddenly, going into spasm, and cutting back the blood flow through them drastically. This tends to occur where the vessel walls are damaged.

Of course, the body fights back. We are equipped with self-repair and maintenance systems of wonderful complexity. But they all depend upon a healthy cardiovascular system to work at their best. And that system itself has the same regenerative capacity, but the factors which cause illness will also block healing. The result is an avoidable decline.

Although many doctors treat the heart as if it becomes diseased independently of the rest of the body, it makes little sense to think of the problem in this way. A healthy heart is just part of a healthy body. Healthy blood vessels deliver plentiful blood to the heart as they do to the limbs, the kidneys, the brain, and every other part of the system. The heart is more susceptible to catastrophic failure, but where the blood is passed through the kidneys, the brain and the eyes, the fine tubes which provide the functional interface are liable to structural failure. The action we can take to protect the heart is precisely the same as that which we take to improve other parts of the system.

While it is possible to view the cardiovascular system as a mechanical/hydraulic system of pipes and pump, we must not forget that the body is far more complex than any machine. Both heart and blood vessels receive inputs from the nervous system, controlling their function and regulating the quantity and content of blood pumped through them. Fear can make us go white and cause the heart to skip a beat; all the parts of the system are affected. Strenuous activity can turn the skin pink and make our hearts pound powerfully. Drugs such as nicotine can alter the responses of all parts of the system at once. It is a highly sensitive and reactive system, supremely adaptable – but it is also susceptible to damage in any or all of its interlinked parts. This is especially true when it is subjected to long-term stresses which tax its capacity to adapt.

One view of the heart disease problem is that this adaptive capacity is being overloaded. The rise in cardiovascular disease began more than a century ago, but it has accelerated dramatically in the last fifty years. Precisely how great the rise has been, and when it began, is uncertain because figures are unreliable for earlier decades. In this heart disease suffers, with most other diseases, from a major failure in our health systems. Although we all have access to doctors and hospitals, the information on exactly what they are treating and how is vague. We do not know how many people are suffering from what, nor do we know enough about the outcome of the treatment they receive to judge its value or effectiveness. Even today, when almost every school pupil has access to a computer that could manage this vital task, the prevalence of low-level manifest-ations of heart disease is not known precisely.

The change in death-rates provides the clearest evidence. But even so, changes in fashion and classification affect diagnoses. What an Edwardian doctor would have called 'old age', today's

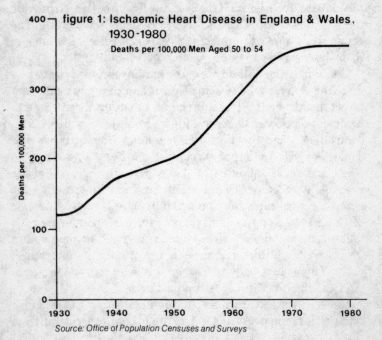

figure 1: Ischaemic Heart Disease in England & Wales, 1930-1980

Deaths per 100,000 Men Aged 50 to 54

Source: Office of Population Censuses and Surveys

specialists will give a precise name to; even when a broader description might often be more appropriate in the case of death being the product of generalised degeneration.

Figures for deaths due to heart attack are the most reliable. These go back to Victorian times, and they reveal a definite increase. Over the course of this century, they have risen roughly four-fold in most Western industrial countries. But this rise has not affected all countries equally, or all groups equally within each country. The pattern of change shows an intriguing picture, one that should tell us a lot about the nature of the stresses that have caused the rise – if we can interpret it.

The most important feature of the rise is a shift down the age-scale. Heart attacks now strike at much younger people than previously, and it is among the younger age-groups that the rise has been greatest. The graph (figure 1) shows how the figures for

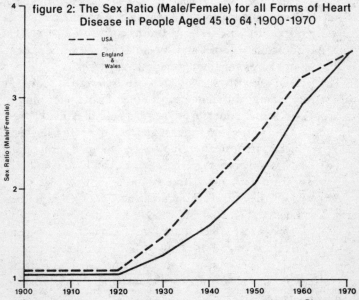

figure 2: The Sex Ratio (Male/Female) for all Forms of Heart Disease in People Aged 45 to 64 ,1900-1970

Source: T.W. Anderson (1976), quoted in Roy Shephard, Ischaemic Heart Disease and Exercise, Croom Helm, 1981

deaths from heart attacks have changed in England and Wales.

The second feature is a change in distribution of heart attack deaths between the sexes (figure 2). Early this century, men and women were roughly equally likely to have heart attacks. Then, in 1920 in the United States, and about 1930 in Britain, men became much more susceptible than women. By 1970 men between forty-five and sixty-four were over three times more likely to suffer fatal heart attacks than women of the same age. Now, in the 1980s, the positions seem to be changing again. Men are becoming slightly less susceptible, and women more so. Women seem to be catching up once more.

For a long time many people believed that heart attacks afflicted mainly the managerial classes. Today the opposite is true. Although people from all groups are liable to fall victim to heart disease, the lowest social classes are disproportionately affected. The death-rate from all causes is higher for the less privileged, and deaths from heart disease are no exception. But there is some evidence that the managerial myth could once have been true; the rise in heart deaths seems to have started among white-collar people, and spread down the social scale to become more common among the less privileged.

The rickety statistics to which we referred produce a differential among different occupations. Labourers, miners, transport workers, builders, and members of the Armed Forces are among the groups who suffer high levels of death from heart disease; metal tradesmen, employers, company directors, technicians, woodworkers, farmworkers, and conveniently, undertakers, are particularly free from it.

Some people live in social circumstances which add to their risk. The isolated, divorced and widowed are highly susceptible to heart attack. Most affected are those who lost their partner while relatively young. But people whose isolation is evident from a lack of association with social groups, such as religious organisations, are also more vulnerable than those who are better integrated.

The variations imply wide differences in susceptibility

between individuals. But the variations between whole populations, between countries, are also great (figure 3). Although the precise details of the league table vary slightly from year to year, there is no doubt that Britain, North America, Northern Europe, with Australia and New Zealand, head the list. The mediterranean countries – France, Greece, Italy and Spain – have a much lower heart disease rate. And most parts of Africa, Asia and Japan have lower rates still. These differences point to the cultural nature of heart disease.

In some countries other manifestations of heart disease are relatively higher than deaths from heart attack. Japan is the outstanding example; strokes are common, heart attacks are not. Perhaps the most interesting and potentially valuable aspect of the inter-cultural variation is the virtual absence of any form of cardiovascular disease in tribal groups which have not been dramatically changed by Westernisation. Such groups are becoming rarer with every decade, but they still exist in the heart of Africa and South America.

In the 1930s both heart and blood vessel disease was extremely rare in Uganda, Tanzania and Kenya. At this time when Western influences were thin on the ground, degeneration that was assumed to be the natural consequence of aging just did not affect these people. Their blood vessels showed no signs of clogging with atheroma, they did not develop high blood pressure, and even in old age they were extremely unlikely to suffer heart attacks. Leg pain and other signs of damage to the major limb arteries occurred only after injury. Damage was inflicted from outside; it did not develop insidiously within their bodies.

Dr Vint was the first British government pathologist to work in East Africa. In 1936 he published the results of a thousand autopsies on Kenyans. Among this thousand were 56 cardiovascular deaths – about a tenth of the number that would be found in a similar series in Britain today. He did not find one heart attack victim, nor signs of damage to the coronary arteries. In the United States today there is evidence that these arteries

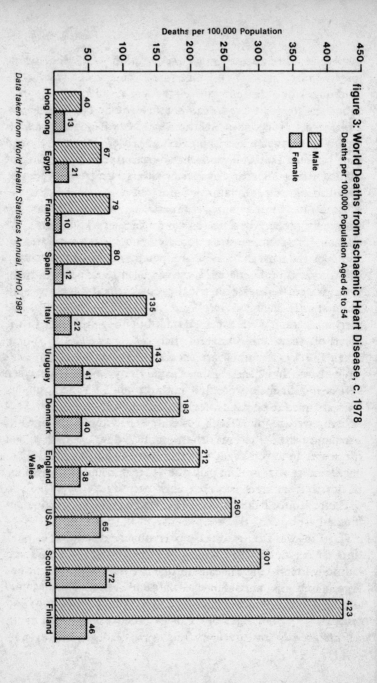

figure 3: World Deaths from Ischaemic Heart Disease, c. 1978
Deaths per 100,000 Population Aged 45 to 54

Deaths per 100,000 Population

Male
Female

Country	Male	Female
Hong Kong	40	13
Egypt	67	21
France	79	10
Spain	80	12
Italy	135	22
Uruguay	143	41
Denmark	183	40
England & Wales	212	38
USA	260	65
Scotland	301	72
Finland	423	46

Data taken from World Health Statistics Annual, WHO, 1981

show signs of damage even among children, and by the age of twenty, forty per cent of Americans have some degree of atheroma.

The first report of coronary heart disease among Ugandans appeared in 1948: one woman among 2,994 autopsies. The first reports of heart attacks striking Africans in Kenya and Tanzania were published in 1968. Even today, heart disease is rare among South African Bantus. In Johannesburg, heart attack death rates are more than fifty times higher in whites than in blacks.

However, this may only reflect the fact that coronary heart disease emerges more slowly than other types of blood-vessel disease. The blood vessels feeding the brain appear to be damaged more quickly by Western influences. In the 1940s, strokes were very rare among Africans. One report on 3000 Ugandan necropsies revealed that only 4 had died of cerebral haemorrhage. But by 1956, eleven per cent of patients admitted to the neurological ward of one Ugandan hospital were suffering the effects of diseased blood vessels to the brain. By 1970, the figure had risen to thirty-four per cent. This rise paralleled a rise in the incidence of high blood pressure among the population; before 1940, hypertension was not a problem for Africans.

Heart disease deaths are not increasing everywhere. In Britain, we are on a high plateau. Deaths from heart and circulatory disease are stable at roughly 300,000 per year. The rise seems to have halted, or at least paused. It could even be beginning to decline. But this still represents more than half of all deaths from all causes each year.

In the United States and Canada the number of heart attack deaths has dropped by about twenty-five per cent since a high peak in 1967. This is very important; it demonstrates that, whether by design or chance, the rate of fatalities can be reduced. Identifying the cause of the decline is not easy; many suggestions, each with some face validity, have been made. But all are as unconvincing in isolation as single causes of the disease.

Finland was until recently the world leader in death and

disability from heart and cardiovascular disease. A massive educational campaign was set up in North Karelia, the Finnish province where deaths were highest. The message spread outside the local area to influence people all over Finland. Many of the eating and behaviour patterns which are known to affect the development of cardiovascular disorders changed for the better. Where once north Karelia stood supreme, the Valleys of south Wales now lead. Will the Welsh follow the Finnish example and in changing their way of life avoid their predictable way of death?

The improvements in the United States, Canada and Finland are cause for optimism. But we should be realistic about their scale and long-term implications. A twenty-five per cent fall in deaths among middle-aged people that follows a much greater rise by no means indicates that the problem has been solved. Death-rates in the United States and Finland are still very high by world standards. They are merely less extreme than they were. Moreover, it is probable that the types of change that have brought these recent benefits are limited in the degree of impact they can have. They are in a real sense superficial modifications.

The change in the progress of the American heart epidemic has been investigated in some detail by Professor Roy Shephard, who commented thus: 'Naturally, many groups, ranging from exercise enthusiasts to cardiac surgeons, have been eager to claim responsibility for this favourable trend.' He then proceeded to evaluate the claims with statistical rigour.

Professor Shephard believes that the decrease in cigarette smoking has made the largest contribution. This reached a peak with sixty-three per cent of the American population smoking in 1955, subsequently dropping to forty-six per cent in 1970. The fall has continued since. Shephard attributes a twelve per cent decrease in heart deaths to this, and thinks it could produce further benefits.

The second largest benefit he believes to be due to increased physical activity. The proportion of physically active people has doubled; cycling, skiing and, of course, running are among the sports that have become much more popular. Even so, the majority of people take only one session a week or less of endurance activity. The decrease in heart deaths attributable to increased activity he estimates at ten per cent. A reduction in animal fat in the average US diet may also have contributed to the fall in deaths. This is not certain because the move away from animal fat began while the epidemic was still rising. What, if any, contribution this change has made is not clear.

Finally, he believes that improvements in treatment may have produced some fall in the heart disease death-rate. Reduction of blood pressure through drug therapy probably reduces deaths from certain types of heart disease, and improved treatment after a heart attack has probably raised survival rates. However, the most marked fall in death-rates has been for acute cases, who often die before treatment can be initiated. The maximum benefit therefore due to medical advances may be of the order of two per cent. But from this gain must be taken the costs. It will be balanced by hazards which lead to rises in death-rates from non-cardiac causes. Drug-induced disease, death due to surgery and infections acquired in hospital are serious drawbacks of all forms of medical and surgical intervention.

The changes recorded in the United States and Finland reflect a growing awareness that heart disease is something we bring upon ourselves. While it is acknowledged that we do this by living in ways that are not appropriate, precisely what this means for any individual is not clear. Cardiologists argue constantly about the relative importance of the various factors that have been implicated as contributors to the heart disease epidemic.

As ever more resources are poured into attempts to solve the heart disease problem, there is a continuing failure to find a convincing answer. A great many 'solutions' are proposed, vigorously attacked and equally vigorously applied by their proponents. Yet there is very little agreement between experts. The perpetual arguments spread confusion among those outside their ranks.

Some experts put their patients on very low fat diets. One eminent cardiologist goes through his hospital ward, marking his patients' notes with the emphatic instruction that they have just as much butter and cream as they want. So what is the relevance of cholesterol? What are we to conclude about dietary causes of heart disease? Another expert devotes pages of his books to the hazards of exercise, the nastiness of jogging and its association with heart attacks. His view is that the personality of the individual is all-important. No amount of activity will save you if you have a heart-attack-prone personality. Others run cardiac rehabilitation clinics in which exercise plays a crucial role in treatment and prevention of the same problem. How can they all be right? And if some are wrong, how do we decide which is which?

Amid such partisan – yet narrowly reasonable – cacophony, even the most concerned individuals are likely to end up with the nihilist conclusion that they might as well get on with their lives, and if the heart attack comes, so let it. There is little point in devoting oneself to strategies that might make matters worse.

Statistical links have been demonstrated between heart attacks and a plethora of physical, behavioural and cultural variables. Many of these interact with one another; some are consequences of others; some make others possible, or are adaptations of others. The whole picture forms a complex tapestry which reflects the totality of our lives. This is why no small selection of features will ever account for all the victims of heart disease. Similarly, no single carefully defined strategy will suit everybody. No blanket regime will offer a final answer. We are looking at the interaction between highly variable individuals and their constantly changing environment. The product of that interaction can be heart disease; but if we understand the process, we can avoid it.

By understanding yourself and your life in relation to the heart disease risk factors, you will be able to achieve a balance. This will allow you to concentrate your efforts at avoiding heart disease in those areas that are relevant to you as an individual. This may seem daunting, but it is not; it is simply a matter of getting to know yourself and your needs.

CHAPTER 2

Why Are We at Risk?

Dost thou think, because thou art virtuous,
there shall be no more cakes and ale?

William Shakespeare *Twelfth Night*

Epidemiologists have for some decades been studying the effects and comparative importance of what have become known as the classical risk factors for heart disease. The popularity of these influences for research and study is based only partly on their predictive value; more important is their ease of measurement. They have been efficiently standardised, so each expert knows what the other is talking about.

The preoccupation with esoteric knowledge permeates all levels of professional concern with heart disease. Medical textbooks devote many pages to such topics as the significance of a deformed T wave or the height of the QRS complex in the electrocardiogram. The problem with this trend is that the usefulness of the knowledge it produces becomes increasingly irrelevant. It is a little like seeking to understand everything about snowflakes when the immediate problem is an avalanche. Nevertheless, many patients are impressed by the shiny machines of the technological approach, almost as if its value was in direct proportion to its incomprehensibility.

This book is not written for people who wish to subordinate themselves to experts. In our view, when we come to rely on technological measures to understand health status, we have given up control of our bodies, and to some degree of our lives. It is more important for each of us to understand why particular things put us at risk, than to know precisely what their effects are. 'Understanding why' puts you in control; 'measuring what' reduces you to the status of a passive observer.

In this chapter we will be looking at certain specific factors which have been linked with heart disease.

Cholesterol

Of the classical risk factors, the most important predictor of death from heart attack is high blood cholesterol. This is why there has been so much concern over cholesterol.

Cholesterol is a lipid, a substance very similar to a fat. Small quantities of cholesterol are always present in the blood. Some of this is derived from the food we eat, dietary cholesterol. Some foods are particularly high in cholesterol, egg yolks, liver, and brains, for instance. Even if our diet contained no cholesterol at all, it would still be present in our blood stream. Cholesterol is manufactured by the liver and by many other tissues of our bodies; it is an important component of every one of our cells, and has essential special functions like insulating our nerve fibres.

It was recognised more than a century ago that people who suffered angina and heart attacks had deposits of a fatty porridge-like substance in the major arteries feeding the heart. When this substance was shown to be cholesterol, the stage was set for the ascendancy of the cholesterol theory of heart disease.

High levels of cholesterol in the blood are associated with the development of atheroma, and with most forms of heart disease. Since the 1930s, atheromatous changes have been seen in greater proportions of the population, and at progressively younger ages. Of 3,000 US Army soldiers below the age of thirty killed in Korea, fifty per cent had some change and twenty-five per cent had marked changes in their coronary arteries. Nor does this only apply to Americans. Of 400 young men in the RAF who died in crashes, thirty per cent showed severe changes, forty-five per cent moderate changes and only twenty-five per cent were completely free from atheroma.

It has recently been discovered that the cholesterol situation is more complicated than previously thought. The hazard posed by cholesterol seems to depend on the chemical carrier with which it journeys around the body. Lipids circulate in the blood in complexes with specialised carrier proteins called lipoproteins. Cholesterol may be carried on various types of lipoproteins, which biochemists separate by their density. Cholesterol is only dangerous if it is bound to low density lipoproteins (LDL). High density lipoproteins (HDL) are protective; they have more protein, less cholesterol. But this differentiation does not make much practical difference. If your blood cholesterol level is high, the chances are that your low density lipoproteins are high too.

Basically, the original cholesterol theory held that people who consumed too much high-cholesterol food were likely to develop high levels of cholesterol in the blood. This dietary cholesterol was deposited in the arteries, particularly where they had suffered slight injury. Such injuries are especially common in the coronary arteries, presumably because of the strain to which they are subjected as they cling to a constantly moving heart.

Localised deposits of cholesterol are known as plaques, and they seem to cause no trouble if they stay intact. However, in Western people, large plaques are liable to degenerate, dying in the centre and breaking down to produce a greasy mess. This is separated from the circulating blood by a cap, but the cap is liable to fail under pressure from the foul mess beneath as the degeneration of the plaque progresses, producing an ulcerated area in the arterial lining. At this point, a blood clot may form on the damaged wall of the artery.

Adherents of the theory explain that cholesterol deposits are liable to thicken, and plaques become more liable to break down, if the individual continues to eat a high cholesterol diet. Eventually, the arteries become clogged. Cholesterol build-up happens first in the coronary arteries, later in other major arteries such as those feeding the legs, but its effects are the same wherever it happens: it blocks the flow of blood to the tissues that need it.

Spasm in the vessels can add to the problem. Arteries are not like garden hoses, they have muscular walls which are capable of dilating or contracting when suitably stimulated by the nervous system. Exactly why spasm occurs is not usually known, but it seems that damaged arteries are more likely to go into spasm. Atheroma builds up in the same parts of the vessel, so the two types of constriction add to each others' effects. Susceptibility to spasm varies markedly from day to day; angina sufferers experience good days, when they can walk for miles, and bad days when a hundred yards will bring crippling pain. Emotional stress and exhaustion make the problem worse.

The blood supply reaching the heart muscle through narrowed coronary vessels may be insufficient to meet its needs, especially when it is working hard. The lack of blood and consequent lack of oxygen delivered to the heart cells, is known as ischaemia. It produces the pain of angina.

If a clot should block the remaining space in a coronary vessel, there will be a sudden and catastrophic reduction in the amount of oxygen available to the heart. This is a heart attack. Parts of the heart muscle die. In their death-throes, some cells may set up electrical abnormalities, which make matters even worse by disrupting the normal pulsing sequence. The living heart muscle becomes disorganised, its pumping action stops. It has been described under these conditions as 'writhing hideously like a mass of worms'.

This phenomenon is known as ventricular fibrillation, and it is the most common reason for sudden death due to heart attack. If normal electrical pulsing can be re-started, as it sometimes can be with heart massage or electric shock, then the person may survive. But this must happen fast, for a fibrillating heart cannot deliver blood to the brain, and the result, very soon, is brain death.

For the most part, the cholesterol theory seems to fit the facts well. Links have repeatedly been shown between blood cholesterol levels and heart disease. In countries where the average blood cholesterol level is high, heart disease is common. In the United States, the blood cholesterol level that is regarded as normal for a middle-aged man – 230 mg/100 ml – is almost twice the average of that in populations in other parts of the world where few people have heart attacks. In Japan, for example, only a minority of people have cholesterol levels above 150 mg/100 ml; and blood cholesterol in 'primitive' communities is even lower. In Mediterranean countries, where heart disease is also uncommon, many people have cholesterol levels as low as 160 mg/100 ml.

Within countries, blood cholesterol levels show reliable associations with heart disease rates. People with the highest levels run the highest risk. About one child in five hundred suffers from a metabolic disorder that results in very high levels of blood cholesterol. They are liable to have heart attacks in their twenties, or even in their teens.

The existence of a link between blood fats and heart disease is undeniable. But proponents of the cholesterol theory have gone further. Many argue that the cause of the problem is dietary cholesterol, that heart attacks are directly caused by blockage of coronary vessels with cholesterol-loaded plaques.

Eating habits do affect cholesterol. But small variations in cholesterol intake – such as those between individuals who eat a fairly typical Western diet, but substitute sunflower margarine for butter and avoid eggs and cream, and others who eat precisely what they fancy – do not seem to produce systematic effects on blood cholesterol. Nor can much of the variation within the population be explained in terms of diet.

In a long-running study of cardiovascular disease among the people of Framingham, a small town in New England, it was found that people whose consumption of cholesterol was below average had exactly similar blood cholesterol levels to those who ate more than the average amount of cholesterol. In another survey in Tecumseh, in the United States, a thousand people were divided into three groups on the basis of their blood cholesterol levels. It was found that the highest group consumed the same quantity of fats of all kinds, and the same total quantity of food, as those in the middle and lowest. There were no significant differences between the three groups in eating habits. In fact, the only consumption measure that did show a significant relationship with blood cholesterol was alcohol intake: the highest cholesterol group drank seventy per cent more than .the lowest. Whether there is a direct causal relationship is another question.

Special cholesterol-reducing diets have been widely used and they can reduce blood cholesterol levels by up to twenty per cent. They do not produce the sort of levels that are normal for population groups whose rates of heart disease are particularly low. And a Catch 22 is revealed in those studies where reduction of blood cholesterol has resulted from replacement of saturated fat in the diet by polyunsaturates. While the death-rate from heart disease does decline somewhat, the overall total death-rate remains unchanged because the mortality from other causes, particularly cancer, rises.

The danger to health does not seem to be affected by the substitution of one fat for another. The trend toward replacing animal fats with processed vegetable fats has been occurring simultaneously with the rise in heart disease. In the United States, the consumption of saturated (mainly animal, but also palm and other vegetable) fats has increased by little more than ten per cent over the course of this century. However, consumption of linoleic acid, a polyunsaturated fat that is thought to play a protective role, has increased to well over double its 1910 level. Apparently this has not had the effects that the diet-cholesterol theorists would have expected. The real problem seems to be that over this period the structure of our diet has changed. In 1910 fats contributed twenty-five to thirty per cent of our calorie input; today they contribute forty per cent at least.

Recent research has added another twist to the story. The crucial question may concern the purity of the fats we eat. At the beginning of this century, middle- and upper-class people ate richer food than most of us do today, and much more of it too, many having four set meals each day. But the food was minimally processed.

Similarly, some cultural groups – the Masai, tall warrior cattle-herders, and Somali herdsmen – have a diet that is very high in cholesterol, but again it is fresh and pure. In all these cases, atheromatous deposits do build up in the blood vessels, but they seem to be harmless. They do not lead to heart attacks and angina. They do not show the characteristic degenerative changes that are found in industrial countries where heart disease is rife.

Experiments with rabbits have confirmed that polluted cholesterol which contains oxidation products – the sort of substance that is to be found in processed foods such as dried eggs and milk – produces the characteristic arterial damage that has been blamed on cholesterol. But when their diet is equally rich in purified cholesterol, they do not suffer arterial degeneration. This line of research is in its infancy, but it may explain the inconsistencies in the evidence against cholesterol. It should make us wonder about chips that are cooked in fat which has been heated and cooled many times.

The diet-cholesterol theorists argue that cholesterol manufactured by the body has different characteristics from dietary cholesterol. When cholesterol from food reaches the blood stream, it is differently packaged, and is much more likely to stick to the walls of blood vessels. This may indeed be true, but whether and why, once deposited, it causes damage is surely the crucial question. The answer could lie in the chemical differences between processed and natural cholesterol.

Whatever the case, there is no doubt that the level of

cholesterol in the blood rises more and faster when we are under stress. The changes due to stress are much greater than those which can be attributed to diet. We shall return to this topic in chapter 5.

Refined Sugar

Other aspects of the Western diet have been implicated in the production of unhealthy blood fat profiles. Refined sugar, that other ubiquitous component of diet in our culture, can also produce a rise in blood cholesterol levels.

This has been demonstrated experimentally both in animals and in man, but the cornerstone of the evidence against refined sugar is epidemiological. In those cultures where sugar consumption is high, blood cholesterol levels and death-rates from heart disease are also high. When sugar consumption rises, heart attack rates rise. And when refined carbohydrates like sugar are excluded from the diet, the risk of heart disease falls.

Professor John Yudkin, author of *Pure, White, and Deadly*, has pointed to a twenty-five-fold rise in sugar consumption in Britain over the past two hundred years. The greatest rise in world sugar production took place between 1938 and 1958, when consumption doubled. For comparison, milk production rose by thirty per cent, meat and grain by fifty per cent. The net effect was a marked increase in the proportion of sugar in our diet. The sharp rise in heart attack rates all over the world in the 1940s and 1950s is not likely to be a coincidence.

This is one result of the industrialisation of food production. Sugar is an ideal product; it has an indefinite shelf-life, and it helps other foods to keep longer. It is added to everything from tinned vegetables to diet foods. It may also be relevant that sugar is often combined with processed fats, in products ranging from ice-cream to soups.

Two surveys carried out by Professor Yudkin provide damning evidence against sugar. One involved a comparison of the eating habits of heart attack victims, people suffering from arterial disease affecting the limbs, and matched controls who did not have symptoms of cardiovascular disease. He found that the groups suffering from cardiovascular disease consumed twice as much sugar as the one that did not. Repeating the survey with more groups of sufferers and non-sufferers, he demonstrated that this finding was quite consistent.

Next, Professor Yudkin ranked countries in terms of heart disease, then compared these ranks with figures for a range of variables suspected to be associated with it. There are some signs of an association with fat consumption, but the match with sugar consumption was much closer. However, the strongest association was with the number of TV sets, once more indicating the danger of an over-simplistic approach to the heart disease problem!

In another experiment, Yudkin fed fourteen healthy students for three weeks on food which included twice as much sugar as the average British diet contains. At the end of this period, ten of the fourteen showed a fall in high density lipoprotein – the blood fat fraction that protects against heart disease.

Diabetes

An additional important link between dietary sugar and heart disease operates through its effects on insulin metabolism. Many experts believe that sugar consumption causes diabetes.

Before considering this aspect, it is important to differentiate between broad types of diabetes. Juvenile onset diabetes is usually caused by a failure of the pancreas to produce insulin. Mature onset diabetes is usually a failure of the cells to respond to the insulin that is still produced; this is the type of diabetes that develops in middle-aged and elderly people. Both types, in turn, are closely associated with cardiovascular disease.

The majority of diabetics die of heart or blood vessel disease, and part of the increase in cardiovascular disease can be explained in terms of a rise in the prevalence of diabetes. Diabetics' blood vessels are much more vulnerable than those of non-diabetics; the frequent complications of diabetes occur because of problems with blood vessels feeding the eyes, feet and kidneys. Blindness, gangrene in the toes and kidney failure are the results.

The consumption of sugar causes an unnaturally sudden and rapid rise in blood sugar. This stimulates the secretion of insulin by the pancreas. Blood sugar levels first rise abnormally high, then fall excessively low as the sugar is moved into the cells of the body under the influence of insulin. This violent see-sawing is called insulin rebound; when the blood sugar drops excessively, the usual response is a craving for sugar. Responding to the craving by eating more sugar puts the blood sugar up once more.

After some years of these wild fluctuations, the cells of the body seem to become resistent to insulin. Normal, or even higher than normal, levels of insulin become insufficient for the metabolism of sugar. The characteristic diabetic state of high blood sugar which spills into the urine is the result. When the cells resist insulin, they cannot derive sufficient energy from the sugar in the blood, and this interferes with their capacity to repair damage. At the same time, there are often disturbances in cholesterol metabolism, producing unusually high levels of blood cholesterol.

Treatment with drugs which reduce blood sugar levels apparently does nothing to protect diabetics from damage to the cardiovascular system. But those who go on the type of low-sugar, low-fat prudent diet that offers some protection against cardiovascular disease find that control over their diabetes is much improved. Indeed, many no longer have abnormal blood sugar levels and are able to discontinue treatment for the diabetes. The fact that identical treatment is effective for both conditions suggests that they are very closely related.

It may be that the fluctuations in blood sugar and insulin levels which result both from eating refined sugar and from established diabetes are directly atherogenic. They upset blood fat levels, causing clogging of the vessels, aided by the interference with damage repair. Possibly, the production of cholesterol is actually an adaptation by the body to unpredictable blood sugar availability. This is one of the many chicken-and-egg problems in cardiovascular disease.

Salt

Salt, like sugar, has become ubiquitous in manufactured foods, and our intake of it has increased enormously. Most people do not realise how much sodium salt they eat. In fact, we consume fifty times as much as our remote ancestors did.

The human body is intended to maintain a precise balance between sodium and its close chemical relation, potassium. While processing and taste habits have pushed up our sodium input, the same forces have produced a three-fold decline in the potassium content of our food. This divergence exaggerates the impact of the increased sodium consumption. In many parts of our bodies, the exchange of sodium and potassium over membranes is essential for their function. Nerves, for example, have a 'sodium pump' which pushes sodium ions one way and potassium ions the other as electrical impulses pass down the nerve. Such a delicate balance is likely to go awry if there is too much of one or the other substance in the body fluid.

So how has the balance of sodium and potassium in our diet gone so far out of kilter? Once again, the answer lies largely in our consumption of processed foods.

The best known source of sodium is common salt. However, table and kitchen salt now provide only about twenty per cent of the sodium in the average Western diet. Processed foods are heavily salted, but they also contain sodium in many other guises: monosodium glutamate (flavour enhancer), sodium bicarbonate (baking powder), sodium nitrite and related preserving salts, sodium caseinate and others. Processing also removes much of the naturally-occurring potassium. Roast beef, for example, contains one-twentieth of the sodium and twice the potassium of corned beef. Corn on the cob contains negligible amounts of sodium; some breakfast cereals contain more, weight for weight, than corned beef. And the potassium content of the corn falls to a third in the transformation to breakfast cereal.

The hazard of this imbalance in relation to cardiovascular disease is that it produces a rise in blood pressure. This may simply be an effect of the body trying to lose excess sodium through the kidneys; but it may be that high blood pressure protects against some effects of the imbalance. Some people seem to be more sensitive than others, but it is nevertheless true that average blood pressure levels over whole populations rise as their consumption of sodium rises. And a low sodium diet can produce a fall in blood pressure. However, even if sodium intake was a major cause of a rise in blood pressure in a particular individual, removing this cause may not be sufficient to reverse the condition once it has become established.

As with dietary cholesterol, relatively small differences in salt intake against a background of massive general over-consumption do not explain wide differences in blood pressure. This should not be surprising; reducing a fifty-fold increase in salt intake to, say, a twenty-fold increase still leaves the system stressed by excessive sodium intake. But for the individual who has deliberately cut salt consumption to less than half it may seem like a great sacrifice for no apparent benefit.

Sodium intake, like the consumption of animal fat in relation to high blood cholesterol, may well play only a small part in the development of high blood pressure. But the contribution it does make may be underwritten by the addictive cycle it induces; salt tends to put up blood pressure, which has some protective advantages, so salt is eaten to keep blood pressure up.

High blood pressure

Whatever its cause, high blood pressure is strongly related to the development of heart disease. The reason is suspected to be a direct mechanical effect: any liquid flowing through a narrow pipe at high pressure is capable of causing damage if the pipe is too weak or the pressure excessively high. Bulges and deformations, which could lead to small tears in a fibrous tube like an artery, occur where there is sufficient elasticity to prevent bursting. These tears become the sites of cholesterol plaques. Small delicate tubes may burst, causing the haemorrhage that is typical of strokes when it occurs in the brain, or the bleeding from the back of the eye that leads to progressive loss of sight in many diabetics.

Viewed in the simplest terms, the heart is a powerful pump and the arteries are the pipes through which it pumps blood. It works at varying rates and pressures according to need, for the quantity of fresh blood required by the tissues clearly varies from time to time. If you are working your muscles hard sawing logs, then those muscles will need a large quantity of blood, supplying plenty of oxygen and nutrients in order to maintain the power output. Your blood pressure will rise, along with your heart-rate and breathing. But if you are slumped in front of the TV, few of your muscles will be doing any work at all. So blood pressure should fall under these circumstances.

Not surprisingly, there are marked variations in blood pressure over the course of the day. These occur not only in response to muscular demand, but also in response to anticipated need. If you are fired up emotionally, your heart-rate and blood pressure will rise to prepare your system for the possibility of a large and immediate demand on the muscles: for the fight or flight response, or to make love to the object of your desire. Or otherwise act in an appropriate manner.

Problems arise when blood pressure is consistently high. This does not produce any obvious symptoms, and it is only likely to be detected if a doctor checks your blood pressure. Blood pressure measurement is carried out using a device called the mercury sphygmomanometer. It involves having a cuff wrapped around one arm and pumped up with air. The pressure in the cuff is gradually reduced, while the doctor listens through a stethoscope to the sound of blood flowing through the main artery of the arm. Characteristic sounds signify the points at which the pressure of air matches the pressure of blood at different points in the heart's pumping cycle. These pressures can be read off the mercury gauge.

The result is a pair of figures: systolic pressure is a measure of the power of the heart's pumping action, and diastolic pressure is the resting pressure in the system between pulses. Blood pressure is described as 'normal' (normotension) when the systolic reading is below 140 mm Hg and the diastolic reading below 90 mm Hg. The units are millimetres of mercury, as in a barometer, and it is written thus: 140/90.

Average blood pressure in healthy Western populations is about 120/80. In general, the lower your usual blood pressure, the longer is your life expectancy, so figures below this are no cause for concern. Only when shock or haemorrhage produces very low levels of blood pressure is there any danger; and even in these cases, the fall in blood pressure is an adaptive advantage, for the amount of bleeding from any wound is reduced.

High blood pressure is said to exist when the figures are 160/95 or above. When this level of blood pressure is consistently found, the person is described as 'hypertensive'. Readings between these extremes – above 140/90 and below 160/95 – are described as 'borderline'.

This division of people into categories according to their blood pressure is an arbitrary one. The majority of people have blood pressures around the lower figures, and decreasing numbers will have higher values. The numbers tail off gradually as the figures become more extreme. The grouping is based on the allocation of cut-off points by observers, in this case, people who worked for the World Health Organisation in the late 1950s. They produced the definitions of normal, borderline and high pressure given here. It is not a true reflection of the actual situation.

In Western countries blood pressure tends to rise with increasing age. This is a major departure from the natural trend. It is not the case in those cultures where sodium is not added to food, or where the amount of salt used is negligible. In Western countries, the risk of cardiovascular disease also rises with age.

Links between blood pressure and cardiovascular disease have been studied over a period of twenty-four years in Framingham. The results of this continuing research show that heart disease is much more common among those who have high blood pressure. The higher the pressure and the longer its duration, the greater the risk. The Framingham researchers divided their study population into five groups on the basis of systolic blood pressure. People in the lowest blood pressure group had readings of less than 120, while those in the highest were over 180. Middle-aged men in the highest group were six times more likely to become heart disease victims than those in the lowest group. The earlier in life the rise in blood pressure had occurred, the more serious was the hazard. Both strokes and heart attacks were linked with high blood pressure. But neither manifestation of disease was found in people whose usual systolic pressure remained below 120.

Other studies have confirmed the general pattern of results produced from the Framingham research, but no others have been quite as detailed, nor have they continued over such a long period of time. Nevertheless, they demonstrate that the consequences of high blood pressure found in Framingham are much the same everywhere. The dietary habits of the populations of Framingham and elsewhere are not likely to provide a complete explanation of the rise in blood pressure, or the epidemic of heart disease which is associated with the high levels of blood pressure which are common in Western populations. Once again we come up against the effects of wider factors, which are discussed in later chapters.

Smoking

Smoking is probably the most dangerous widespread social habit that people choose to indulge. There can be very few who still fail to appreciate that cigarette smoke causes lung cancer, but many do not realise that the number of heart attack deaths linked with cigarettes could be much greater. Cigarettes have been most consistently linked with circulatory problems affecting the legs and with sudden death, especially among younger men. They do not seem to increase the risk of stroke. The reasons for this particular pattern of effects are not yet fully understood, but enough pieces of the jigsaw have been identified for a fairly clear picture to emerge.

Tobacco smoke has two components which are important in the production of cardiovascular disease: nicotine and carbon monoxide. Both are rapidly absorbed from the lungs of smokers who inhale. All smokers have detectable levels of carbon monoxide in their blood, but in those who smoke cigarettes it is six times higher than in pipe or cigar smokers. Within minutes of lighting a cigarette, the coronary arteries are flooded with nicotine. Nicotine mobilises the hormone adrenalin from the adrenal glands into the blood stream. Adrenalin has two effects on the heart muscle; it makes it work harder and faster, and it increases the oxygen demand. This produces one part of the smokers' risk.

Carbon monoxide is a powerful poison which combines with haemoglobin in the blood, pushing oxygen out. Unlike oxygen, it does not readily separate from the haemoglobin to permit the exchange of gases in the lungs. In consequence, the whole body is deprived of oxygen, and each breath a smoker takes is less effective. So at the time when the heart needs more oxygen, less is available. Heart attacks are the consequence of inadequate oxygen supply to the heart muscle. It is entirely predictable that cigarette smokers are more likely to die suddenly from heart attacks. However, it was observed in Framingham that this rise in susceptibility to heart attacks was apparent only in younger men. Around the age of sixty, the effect disappeared. It has been suggested that the great increase in heart attack rates with age may have obscured the constant increment due to smoking.

Nicotine is a remarkable drug with a two-phase action. First it stimulates, then it tranquillises. As it is absorbed from the lungs, it makes the heart beat faster and harder, and it can stimulate premature beats. Many smokers and ex-smokers will be familiar with the rush that comes as they pull on the first cigarette of the day: the crashing heart-beat and even slight clouding of consciousness. Then follows the sense of calm alertness that keeps so many people addicted to the drug.

Nicotine is not only a powerful tranquilliser; it is unique among tranquillisers in that it improves concentration. Thus it is ideally suited to helping people to cope with the demands of life in Western industrialised society. But as with other potent drugs, the benefits come with heavy costs. One such cost is the direct effect on the heart muscle: a tendency to overreaction, and reduced stability of the heart-beat. The second is constriction of small blood vessels throughout the body, producing a temporary increase in blood pressure. This action on small vessels may explain the well-documented link between cigarette smoking and leg pain. Direct damage to the lining of blood vessels probably adds to the problem, and the possibility of cholesterol plaque formation.

Catastrophic danger is at its greatest while the individual is actually smoking. But between cigarettes, heavy smokers suffer from reduced blood oxygen levels, and the effect of this is amplified by damage to the lungs themselves. The results are chronic breathlessness and lack of stamina – and, of course, the chance of death from lung cancer.

Caffeine

Another stimulant which has been linked with heart disease is so common that we generally do not think of it as a drug. This is caffeine, the stimulant component of coffee and, to a lesser degree, tea. Although no clear link has been demonstrated between the physiological effects of caffeine and the development of heart disease, the statistical association between heart attacks and the consumption of five or more cups of coffee a day is strong. However, such high levels of coffee-drinking are particularly characteristic of cigarette smokers; and when account is taken of this, the impact of coffee as an independent contributor to heart attacks is much less clear.

Oral contraceptives

The risk for women from cigarette smoking is much less than it is for men, but they may face a special danger which men do not share: oral contraception. Oral contraceptives produce an increase in many of the physiological indices which are linked with cardiovascular disease. They cause a rise in blood pressure, increase the tendency of the blood to clot, and change the blood fat profile of the women who take them.

Dr Valerie Beral has studied the statistical association between oral contraceptive use and death-rates among women under forty-five. She found that fatal heart attacks and strokes among young women were falling in most countries during the 1950s, but they began to rise again in countries where the 'Pill' became popular in the 1960s.

Other researchers compared the contraceptive history of women who died or were admitted to hospital with cardiovascular problems with matched groups suffering from other types of illness. They discovered that there is a real and marked increase in susceptibility to heart and circulatory disease which persists for a decade and more after Pill use has stopped. The longer women take the Pill, and the higher the dose of hormones in the particular type they take, the greater is the risk. Smoking and increasing age compound the hazard.

Precisely how serious this hazard may be with the low-dose

forms of Pill in use today, is a controversial question. Dr Beral and some others believe that the Pill could be responsible for as many as one death in four among users. Many doctors would dispute this figure. But few would deny that the risks of embolism, heart attack and stroke are increased at least three times for current users, and may be trebled for past users who took the Pill for ten years or more. Since the death-rate among women of this age is low, even such a massive increase in risk would tend to go unnoticed in the community.

One of the disturbing familiar effects of the Pill that particularly affects young women is its impact on body weight. Some undoubtedly continue to smoke cigarettes in order to minimise weight gain. This tendency, generalised throughout the population of Pill-takers and others, confuses the effect of weight on the risk of cardiovascular disease.

Severe obesity

While body weight is a function of height, body build and type, sex and degree of muscular development, there would be relatively little variation between different people of the same height if body fat could be removed. For decades, it has been known that the risk of heart disease rises with increasing weight. Insurance companies have developed detailed tables of the reduction in life expectancy produced by obesity. Body fat is likely to be the crucial variable, affecting blood pressure, blood cholesterol and susceptibility to cardiovascular disease.

Severe obesity makes any activity more of a strain, particularly if compounded by physical incompetence. Carrying any heavy weight, even walking becomes a struggle, and the demand it makes on the heart is noticeably greater. Fat is better distributed on the body than shopping bags or whatever other weight we may choose to carry, but even so, severely overweight people will be puffing and panting long before their leaner peers. So they are more likely to suffer the problems that result from inadequate oxygen supply to the tissues. If overweight people avoid stressing their bodies by avoiding physical activity, then circulatory efficiency will tend to decline. A dangerous cycle of degeneration is easily set up, just by doing nothing.

This may be part of the explanation for the rise in blood pressure with increased weight. It has been well established that blood pressure levels over whole populations vary systematically with average weight. It is also clear from studies such as Framingham that people with high blood pressure are heavier than those whose blood pressure is lower.

Another contributing factor may be the increased volume of tissue that must be provided with blood, which would have to be pumped harder to penetrate further. Whatever the cause of the relationship, it has been demonstrated that an average fall in systolic pressure of 16 mm Hg can be achieved with a weight loss of 3 kg (about 7 lb) or more.

If the obese person takes up physical activity, or if he or she is subjected to stress sufficiently intense to cause the release of adrenalin, which mobilises fat, a second type of hazard emerges. The quantity of fat released into the blood under the influence of adrenalin is proportional to the total body fat. So obese people's blood fat level rises higher than it would if they were lean. When the level of free fatty acids in the blood rises too high, the heart tends to beat erratically and with less force. Because of this it is essential that overweight people increase their activity levels carefully, and with a clear understanding of what they are doing. More of this in chapter 8.

Although body weight is the variable most easily measured, it is less important than the distribution and quality of that weight, the actual shape of the body. It is intuitively obvious that the well-muscled athlete is not likely to run as high a risk of disease as the sedentary individual of the same height and weight, and indeed there is considerable evidence to support this proposition. But it is not simply a question of whether the weight is muscle or fat; the position of the fat deposits is important too.

A recent survey, part of a long-term study of men in Göteborg in Sweden, revealed that conventional measures of fatness such as the body mass index, which relates height to weight and expresses the relationship of the two as a single function, and skinfold thickness measured with special callipers on the arm and body, were poor predictors of heart attacks and strokes. One reason for this was the very large variability between the individuals in each of the groups. There is so much overlap that populations only appear to differ reliably when very large numbers are studied. Information of this type is effectively useless for making predictions about individuals.

As far as cardiovascular disease is concerned, the crucial measure proved to be paunch size. People who have hips of much the same size as their waists, or who have lost their waist so completely that the belly is bigger than the hips, are the most susceptible. The actual girth of waist or hip was found to have no independent predictive value: it was the relationship between the two measures that proved crucial. Interestingly, the people who were most likely to succumb to cardiovascular disease were those who were relatively light for their height, but who had no waists. The lowest risk group were quite heavy, but slim at the midriff. So it seems that muscular development, which results in heavier limbs and shoulders, is protective in more ways than one.

The Göteborg team found that the protective effects of a slim waist in relation to hips was even more marked among women than men. Very few women have a waist measurement the same or larger than their hips. But this minority group suffers an exceptionally high rate of heart disease. By contrast, a woman whose waist is just two thirds of her hip size, like the 36-24-36 ideal, is extremely unlikely to have a heart attack or a stroke. Her life expectancy is considerably greater than her cylindrical sisters'. After middle age many women spread rather quickly around the midriff. Paunches, rare among young women, begin to accumulate with the passing years. It appears to be no coincidence that heart deaths also rise fast among these women.

As aging women develop male patterns of fat distribution, they run increasing risk of male patterns of illness.

Genetics

Of course, body shape has an important genetic component, as indeed does susceptibility to heart disease. There are two main views about genetics, and both are correct, up to a point. Where that point is will vary from genetic characteristic to characteristic, and from individual to individual.

The predominant view is that our genes are immutable, carrying risk factors that we can do nothing to change because they are built into every cell of the body. All we can do about genetic susceptibility is to recognise it as it applies to each of us, and to take special care to live in such a way as to reduce any extra risk we may suspect we run.

The second, more hopeful, view is that genes represent a potential. To a greater or lesser degree you can control whether or not the potential of your genes is fulfilled. For instance, if your genetic potential is to be very tall, you will not fulfil that potential unless you are fed appropriately. This is particularly true of genes which indicate tendency; a tendency to develop a paunch does not have to be fulfilled, you can control it by being sufficiently active.

It is a curious feature of cardiovascular disease that the mother's health in this respect is considerably more important than the father's. Whether this reflects some factor which operates while we are in intimate contact with the mother's blood and hormone supply as we develop over nine months in the womb, or whether there is some sex-linked component in susceptibility, is not known.

Equally, the relative contributions of childhood environmental influences and of genetic predisposition have not been convincingly separated. However, in practical terms it makes little difference to us as adults; our childhood is as fixed as our genes, once it is past. We can but hope that we, as parents, do not expose future generations to the same level of cardiovascular disease as we now face.

CHAPTER 3

Assess Your Risk 1

And so, from hour to hour, we ripe and ripe,
And then, from hour to hour, we rot and rot,
And thereby hangs a tale.

William Shakespeare *As You Like It*

Everyone runs some risk of cardiovascular disease. Like Gregory in the first chapter, we are all working our way through a minefield littered with risk.

Certain risk factors will be very important for some people, but they will not be crucial for everyone. Frequent surveys have shown no more than about thirty per cent of cases of heart disease can be associated with classical risk factors. The more subtle factors which we discuss later will make a greater contribution to the overall hazard for most people.

At this level there will be wide variability. Our personal risk may be so slight as to be negligible, or so high that immediate action is imperative. Most people will fall somewhere in the middle. The questionnaire in this chapter will enable you to assess the risk caused by the factors immediately within your control. By acting appropriately, you can reduce the risk you run to a minimum, and create the background for improving your heart life and general health.

The adaptability of the human body presents a problem; we

can tolerate astonishing levels of damage to the heart and blood vessels without obvious signs. The disease conditions emerge long after the initiating causes, there is an unpredictable time delay. It may be years or decades; in any case, we cannot afford to wait until symptoms emerge before taking action to keep our hearts healthy.

Because of this long incubation period, most of the influences which make us so frighteningly susceptible to it may have to act for decades before they produce any effects that can be detected without a post-mortem. The last thing anyone wants is for the pathologist to find out about massive degeneration after the opportunities for action are all past. We must face the threat of heart disease and take steps to prevent it occurring when that action seems unnecessary.

This is not to say that all is lost if you begin to suffer symptoms. Under these circumstances the damage is almost always reversible, but obviously the task is going to be more difficult and the risk of sudden and serious failure in the system is considerably greater. If you do have symptoms, the action you take to reduce your risk will have positive benefits and could well remove the symptoms eventually. It is particularly important under these circumstances that you understand how each risk factor fits into the total pattern of your situation. There is a section at the end of the chapter designed to give guidance on the importance of possible symptoms.

Many of the influences that contribute to the risk of heart disease may lie a little deeper. They will require assessment of your wider way of life: your attitudes, your behaviour, the way you interact with those closest to you. These aspects will be examined in chapters 5 and 6.

The contribution each factor is likely to make to your total risk rating will be your score. For some habits, such as smoking, the effects shown up in statistical studies of cardiovascular disease are not simple. They seem to be more important for one sex than the other, or at particular ages. The effects are slightly different on different types of cardiovascular disease; some risk factors have only been linked with heart attacks, others may cause more generalised damage. Our scoring system allows for this, but it does mean that it has to be quite complicated.

Go through this chapter carefully, with paper and pencil, building up your risk profile as you go. In addition to paper and pencil, you will need honesty; the aim is not for a high or low score for its own sake, but truth for your sake. As you answer the questions, you will build up a score to be entered in two columns 'A', and 'B'. When any habit is associated with a less than average risk of cardiovascular problems, it will have a minus score. Subtract from your score as appropriate. If your habits tend to be protective rather than hazardous, you will build up a negative total. Make sure that you answer those questions that apply to you, and avoid those that do not. Instructions to note will be given in brackets, eg (men only). The symbol < means less than (as < 4oz, less than 4oz).

Caution: When you have finished this chapter do not rush out with your new-found knowledge and start working on your risk profile. Remember this is only the first part of a complex and highly individual picture. Overreaction at this stage could do more harm than good. Wait until you have got a sound overview of your total situation. Your patience will be rewarded. There are, of course, some exceptions. You can give up sugar today, totally and for ever, and unless you are an insulin-dependent diabetic, the effects will be entirely beneficial. You can cut down on the fat you eat, if need be, tomorrow. Your risk level is likely to go down, without any added hazards or any need for caution. You can decide not to smoke any more, and not put the dreaded day of withdrawal from the weed off any longer.

But you still need to see how all these things fit in with the general, wider pattern of your life, so that you do not inadvertently increase one type of risk by an unwise approach to reducing another. Very often, our actions are adaptations that allow us to cope with underlying problems. If we kick away the crutches that support us without first learning how to stand without them, we court heart disease. Care is needed at every level when dealing with this problem.

Diet

Fat Content

High blood cholesterol levels may be linked with a large proportion of saturated fat in the diet. This type of fat is found in animal products, including dairy produce, eggs and meat – even lean meat – and some foods of vegetable origin, especially hard fats such as coconut oil. Vegetable oils, such as sunflower, olive, safflower and corn oil, do not cause cardiovascular problems; these contain polyunsaturated fats.

(Score 1 in your A column for each of the following foods if you normally eat the quantity specified; if you eat double, score 2 and so on, as appropriate. If you eat less, score 0.)

High cholesterol foods:

		A
eggs	2 per day	+1
cheese (except low fat cottage)	4 oz per day	+1
milk (except skimmed)	2 pints per day	+1
meat	8 oz per day	+1

Other fatty foods:

fried foods (except vegetables)	2 portions per week	+1
chips	2 portions per week	+1
take-away meals (except vegetables)	2 per week	+1

Carbohydrates

The important discrimination to make here is between refined carbohydrates, particularly sugar, and unrefined carbohydrates.

The former, usually as white sugar, are found in most processed and manufactured foods. The latter are found in wholefoods – wholemeal bread and pasta, fresh fruit, brown rice, unpeeled potatoes and other vegetables. Refined carbohydrates increase the risk you run; unrefined carbohydrates tend to be neutral or to decrease the risk.
(Take an average day for your score.)

	A
sugar in drinks: normally added	+1 per teaspoon
soft drinks (except slimmers')	+1 per glass
cakes, biscuits, puddings	+1 per portion
sweets, chocolates, jam, honey	+1 per ounce total
sweetened breakfast cereals	+1 per portion

(If you deliberately choose wholefoods, wholemeal bread and so on, consistently avoiding refined foods, add up your score so far and halve it. Carry the new total forward.)

Salt Balance

The type of salt that can worsen cardiovascular problems contains sodium. This means not only table salt and salt used in cooking (sodium chloride), but also salts used in food processing and manufacture. Balancing sodium in the diet is potassium; this is found in fresh fruit and vegetables, but it is largely lost in cooking. Processing food also removes potassium.

For a healthy cardiovascular system, we need to keep our potassium levels higher, and our sodium levels lower, than is normally the case. When your diet has a healthy balance, you will tend to find most restaurant foods, frozen and other precooked dishes and products such as commercially prepared soups, far too salty. When these types of food taste just right to you or – worse – when you add salt to them, you have taught your taste buds to expect an unnaturally high sodium intake. This increases your cardiovascular risk by raising blood pressure.

Pick *one* of the following:

	A
Generally I prefer:	
salty foods	+2
most foods as they are	+1
foods less salted	—1 (remember to subtract from your score)

Score the following on the basis of your normal habits:

	A
Chinese meals (eaten twice weekly)	+1
fresh fruit: <4 oz or 1 piece per day	+1
fresh fruit: 4 oz or 1 piece per day	0
fresh fruit: 8 oz or 2 pieces per day	−1
fresh fruit: more than 12 oz per day	−2
raw vegetables/salads: 2–4 oz per day	−1
raw vegetables/salads: over 4 oz per day	−2

Caffeine

A high consumption of coffee is associated with increased risk of heart attack.
(Score figures marked with asterisks in your B column. From now on scores will be headed A and B, so make sure they go in the right totals!)

coffee (except de-caffeinated):

	B
4–8 cups per day	+1*
over 8 cups per day	+3*

Alcohol

High alcohol consumption is more common among heart attack victims, but seems to bear no relationship to other forms of cardiovascular disease.

(Count in units of $\frac{1}{2}$ pint of beer, cider, lager; per glass of wine, sherry, etc; per measure ($\frac{1}{5}$ gill) spirits.)

	B
0–3 units per day	0*
4–5 units per day	+1*
6 or more units per day	+3*

Drinking Water

Various surveys have revealed a link – still unexplained but probably genuine – between the hardness of the drinking water and death rates from cardiovascular disease.

	A
tap water hard, unsoftened	−1
tap water soft	+1

Medical Measurements

Our dietary and other habits affect both the content of our blood and the pressure at which it is pumped around the body. Two measurements have particular predictive value for the assessment of risk of cardiovascular disease: blood pressure and blood cholesterol level.

Unless you have been through a thorough medical examination in recent months you will not know these figures. If you are concerned that you could be at high risk, it may be worth while finding out how you rate in these measurements. Blood pressure is relatively easy, and painless, to measure. Some pharmacists offer a blood pressure measurement service. Any doctor is capable of doing it, and you could approach your general practitioner.

If your blood pressure is found to be high, your doctor is likely to want to treat this symptom. You should decide on what to do on the basis of your trust in your doctor, your knowledge of yourself and your reactions to drugs, and information on the drugs currently in use given in chapter 4.

Blood pressure measurements can give valuable feedback about the effectiveness of the action you take to improve your heart life. In the United States many families have their own sphygmomanometer (the device which, with a stethoscope, is used to measure blood pressure). We would not advise you to go this far!

Caution: Blood pressure measurements are variable. If you do keep a record of your blood pressure, you should if possible get the same person to do it for you every time to minimise variations outside yourself.

If you have the figures, this is how to use them. If not assume an average, that is score 0. If at the end you find you are high risk, or marginally so, get it checked and put the figure in.

Blood Pressure

Blood pressure measurement has been explained in chapter 2. Except in very rare types of disease which affect a small proportion of mainly geriatric patients, diastolic and systolic measures are closely related, and we need to take account of only one of the two. The following figures refer to the higher figure only, i.e. systolic blood pressure.

(If you know that your blood pressure has been consistently above a particular level for five years or more, you should double the figure given. Men should also add the appropriate B score to that total. Women use A only.)

Systolic blood pressure (mm Hg):

	A	B (men only)
less than 109	−3	−2*
110–129	−1	−1*
130–149	0	0*
150–169	+1	+1*
170–189	+3	+2*
over 190	+6	+4*

Blood Cholesterol

Blood cholesterol, like blood pressure, changes in response to stress. Measurement requires giving a little blood, usually via your doctor. Both are reflections of the way your body reacts to the way you live your life. So although these are useful measures in that they are the most effective predictors of heart life available, we do not believe that most people should make a great effort to find out what they are. The time would be better spent taking positive action to increase heart life.

For those who do have the figures, here is what they mean in terms of risk. (If you do not have the figure, continue as for blood pressure: score 0 and reassess once you have finished. Women add A and B scores to their respective totals. Men double both A and B scores before adding to theirs.)

(The units are mg/100ml):

	A	B
less than 180	−2	−2*
180–219	0	0
220–239	0	+1*
240–259	+1	+2*
260–279	+2	+4*
over 280	+3	+6*

Age

As people age in Western countries, their risk of cardiovascular disease increases, with heart attack risk arising earlier in life than other forms of vascular disease.

(As the pattern of changing risk with age is slightly different for men and women, the following table is divided into two parts by sex. Add both A and B to your total scores.)

Age in years:	*Men*		*Women*	
	A	B	A	B
less than 30	−4	0*	−4	−2*
30–39	−2	+1*	−3	−1*
40–49	−1	+2*	−1	0*
50–59	0	+4*	0	+1*
60–69	+2	+6*	+2	+3*
70–79	+4	+6*	+4	+4*
over 80	+6	+6*	+7	+4*

Body Type and Build

Some aspects of body type and build affect cardiovascular risk. The proportion of fat in the body is an important variable, but not the only one to be considered.

Height:	A
short: men under 5′ 7″, women under 5′ 2″	+1
medium: men 5′ 7″–5′ 11″, women 5′ 2″–5′ 6″	0
tall: men over 5′ 11″, women over 5′ 6″	−1

Skinfold thickness

Find the point at your side, just below your waist, where you can feel the top of the pelvic girdle, your hip bone. Pinch a fold of relaxed flesh between your finger and thumb, and estimate the thickness of the double layer of skin and subcutaneous fat you are holding. This is the distance between your finger and thumb. Women should have more subcutaneous fat than men.

	A
lean: men under ½″, women under 1″	−1
standard: men ½″–1″, women 1″–2″	0
overweight: men 1″–2″, women 2″–3″	+1
obese: men over 2″, women over 3″	+2

Paunchiness (men)

Measure girth around your navel (length N), then measure the girth around your hips about 4″ below the navel (length H).

	A
navel smaller than hips (N< H)	0
lengths N and H within ½″ of each other	+2
navel ½″ or more larger than hips (N > H)	+6

Paunchiness (women)

Measure your waist, half way between the top of your hip bone and the bottom of your lowest rib – normally the narrowest part of the trunk. Measure your hips at the broadest point. Then subtract the waist measurement from the hip measurement to obtain a figure for the difference in inches.

	A
hip/waist difference over 10″	−3
difference 8″–10″	−1
difference 6″–8″	0
difference 4″–6″	+2
difference 2″–4″	+4
difference less than 2″	+8

Physical Activity

Activity level has a major effect on the sort of weight you carry. Higher levels of physical activity help the cardiovascular system to remain generally more efficient.

Walking

How far do you walk in the average week?

	A
0–1 mile	+2
1–2 miles	+1
2–4 miles	0
4–8 miles	−1
8–14 miles	−2
14–20 miles	−4
over 20 miles	−6

Household/labouring

Which of the following activities occupy 30 minutes or more of your average week? (Add other equally strenuous activities as appropriate. Strenuous activity makes you breathe hard!)

Stair climbing; digging; lifting heavy objects; sawing logs by hand; lawn mowing or rolling without motorised tools.

(Subtract 1 from your A score for each ½ hour session of such activity.)

Sports

Which of the following (or similar strenuous sports, ones which make you sweat!) do you practice regularly?

Running; swimming; tennis; aerobic dance; squash; football; skipping; rowing; weight training.

Total time occupied by vigorous sporting activity:

	A	B
0 to 20 minutes per week	0	0*
20–40 minutes per week	−1	−1*
40–90 minutes per week	−3	−4*
over 90 minutes per week	−4	−2*

Golf; cricket; bowls; curling; croquet; sailing (or other intermittent activities):

	A
0–40 minutes per week	0
40–90 minutes per week	−1
over 90 minutes per week	−2

Sports/strenuous activity regularly enaged in at age 20, subsequently dropped:

Sporting history (men over 30 only)

	B
2 hrs + per week	+3*
1–2 hours per week	+2*
less than 1 hour's sport per week at 20	0*

Smoking

Smoking increases the risk of cardiovascular disease significantly if the smoke is inhaled. Therefore cigarettes are much more closely associated with heart deaths than cigars or pipes. However, the cigarette smoker who turns to cigar or pipe smoking often inhales, making these habits dangerous to this group. Men are much more susceptible to the hazards of smoking than women unless they are taking oral contraceptives. However, the effects of smoking seem to disappear with age. The particular hazard is sudden death from heart attack.

(Men between 30 and 45 years should multiply the added heart attack risk, column B, by 3. Women taking oral contraceptives and men aged 45 to 55 should multiply column B scores by 2.)

Cigarettes (all current smokers):

	A	B
0–10 per day	0	0*
10–20 per day	0	+1*
20–30 per day	+1	+2*
30+ per day	+3	+3*

Cigars/pipe (ex-cigarette smokers only):

	A	B
¼ oz tobacco or 3 cigars or more per day	+1	1*

Family Background

Family history allows you to make some judgement of the possibility that you may have a genetic susceptibility to cardiovascular problems. Alternatively you may be particularly resistent to them. The fate of parents or grandparents are not grounds for making strong assumptions, but they do affect the total risk picture. However, the fact that our forebears did not suffer from heart disease is less useful for prediction than if they did, because the rise in cardiovascular problems is such that people with no family history of this type of disease are now falling victim to it.

(Score 0 for any classification other than the following:)

Parents

	A
both parents lived over 75 years	−2
father dead, cardiovascular disease, 50–70 yrs	+1
father dead, cardiovascular disease, under 50	+2
mother dead, cardiovascular disease, 60–75 yrs	+2
mother dead, cardiovascular disease, under 60	+3
mother dead, cardiovascular disease, under 50	+4
either parent died (any cause) before you were 14	+2

Grandparents:

	A
grandfather died, cardiovascular disease, under 50	+1
grandmother died, cardiovascular disease, under 60	+1

Medical History: treatment and conditions

Childhood Diseases

Add 2 points to your 'B' score if you have ever suffered from scarlet fever or rheumatic fever.

Diabetes

Diabetics run a higher risk of all types of cardiovascular problem than non-diabetics. The risk is associated with the duration of the diabetes.

(The following point scores are for men. The risk posed by diabetes is much greater for women. They should multiply the scores in the table below by 3.)

	A
clinically diagnosed diabetes: duration 0–5 years	+3
clinically diagnosed diabetes: duration 5–10 years	+5
clinically diagnosed diabetes: duration over 10 years	+7

Treatment for Diabetes

The use of tablets to reduce blood sugar increases the risk of cardiovascular disease. Diabetics who take these drugs should add 1 extra point to each of their scores for every 4 years they have been using them.

Chronic Conditions requiring long-term treatment with steroids

Drugs such as hydrocortisone, prednisolone and betamethasone, prescribed mainly for asthma, serious allergic conditions and rheumatic disease increase susceptibility to heart disease. If you take drugs belonging to this group, you should have been given special warnings about them, and you may not be able to stop taking them.

(Add 1 point to your A score for every 2 years of use.)

Oral Contraceptives

Current users of oral contraceptives should add 1 point to their B score for every 2 years of use.

Ex-users of oral contraceptives may have some increased risk. Those who gave up taking the Pill 0–10 years ago should add 1 point to their B score for every 4 years of use. Those who gave up more than 10 years ago should add 1 point for every 8 years' use.

Current smokers should double these figures. There is evidence of interaction between the hazards of smoking and the use of oral contraceptives.

Calculating Your Score

At this point, you should have two totals, A and B. A scores are for general cardiovascular risk, and B for extra heart attack risk. Add A to B to get total C. As a separate calculation, add together all your minus points to arrive at your P score (ignore the minus sign). You will need your A, C and P scores to work out your personal strategy in chapter 8, so keep a note of them.

These figures can only be rough guides. We have worked out an average risk estimate for types of illness that do not necessarily occur together. The risk estimate does not differentiate between cerebrovascular risk (the risk of stroke and other types of brain damage due to failure or blockage of the blood circulation to parts of the brain) and the risk of peripheral vascular disease (failure of the circulation in the limbs).

It also assumes that the risk you run of stroke, for example, is less than the risk of heart attack. For some people, this assumption is not valid. Women over the age of seventy-five, for example, are more likely to suffer strokes than heart attacks; and certain individuals, especially those with very high blood pressure, are more likely to have strokes at any time after middle age.

No self-administered questionnaire can allow for the whole range of individual variation without becoming impossibly cumbersome. And the prediction of cardiovascular risk is not so precisely worked out that any questionnaire, even the most complicated, is capable of giving an accurate figure for each individual who uses it. It is only possible to offer a broad judgement of risk. If it could be said that you run a fifty-fifty risk of heart attack in the next ten years, this still means that nobody can say whether you actually will or will not have that heart attack! The chances are equal both ways.

So when you think about the implications of your risk score, bear these provisos in mind. Remember that the figure so far reflects only part of the picture. At this point, you cannot justify confidence or horror. However, your score may signify a need for action to reduce the impact of these risk factors.

If your total C score was:

−20 or better

You are well aware that your lifestyle choices are not likely to predispose you to cardiovascular disease. You eat prudently, you are exceptionally physically active. If problems arise for you, they will not originate from harmful indulgence, but from your tendency to push yourself too hard.

Your score may reflect the fact that you have all the advantages as far as heart disease is concerned. Perhaps you're young, fit and female, just totting up your score out of curiosity. Is that your situation? Check out chapters 5 and 6. If your score remains low – then give this book to somebody who needs it more than you do!

Between −20 and −5

Your age, condition, and the combination of consumption and lifestyle choices that you make produce a level of cardiovascular risk that is comfortably below average in the Western industrialised world. This score reflects only a part of the picture, but that part looks fine.

−5 to +10

You fall into the borderline group for first-level risk factors. There are two ways of reaching this point. You may be a basically healthy individual who does not do enough to enhance your chances of living a long and healthy life. If you recognise yourself in that description, go back over the questionnaire, picking up the sections where your score builds up. Then think about your habitual level of physical activity. Are you letting your cardiovascular system degenerate through underuse?

A second type of person also falls into this group. You are likely to be making the most healthy choices available to you all down the line – but be hampered by misfortune, age or disease. By doing everything you can to reduce your level of cardiovascular risk, you are also choosing a way of life that will enhance your general health, at the same time minimising the impact of the disadvantages that you cannot avoid.

Whatever your problems, the most effective long-term solution is the same: you need to endeavour to live in the way that best meets the basic requirements of human beings. So the general rules of eating and activity which protect against heart disease will also protect against other types of physiological failure.

Up to this point, we have not dealt with the other dimensions which are particularly crucial for those whose health is not all that they would wish. The issues of meeting our needs for love, involvement, relaxation and intangibles, like hope, form the subject-matter of later chapters.

10 to 30

You are entering the risk zone of heart disease. Things will get worse if you carry on living the way you have. You may be perfectly healthy, but you are taking unnecessary chances, trusting to a system which may not be capable of taking as much abuse as you hope. Heart disease develops slowly. Act now, and you could abort the ill-effects of years of unsuitable lifestyle.

30 to 50

You may well be aware of damage that has already been done to your body. Most likely, the flabby look of your body is mirrored by the furred-up condition of your arteries. Perhaps you are already suffering from diabetes, a bowel condition, cardio-vascular symptoms or other overt evidence of a way of life that leaves much to be desired.

The fact that you have completed this questionnaire shows that you are sufficiently concerned about the risks you are running to be looking for ways of reducing them. Study the rest of this book and map out your plan of action. You can reduce your risk score – and it is imperative that you do so, without delay.

Over 50

You should not need to be told that your risk level is very high. If you are not already suffering symptoms, it is surprising. You are very unfit indeed, and you have good reason to worry about the onset of cardiovascular disease.

Some of your problems might arise from your everyday habits. When your metabolism is thrown out of balance by sugar or the stress of unsuitable diet, when inactivity produces a chronic state of sluggishness, when you keep yourself going with drugs of all sorts, you are not likely to end up feeling particularly good. Changing your lifestyle will not only make you feel fitter, it will enhance the pleasure of life.

You may think that giving up smoking or sugar, reducing your alcohol consumption and building up your level of habitual physical activity are miserable options which will make your life even more unpleasant than it is. Far from it! You will find that you become capable of much greater enjoyment. You will find that your food tastes better with an appetite. Your whole system feels better when you treat it right. Life will be much more fun when you are fit enough to enjoy it – and you can get fitter.

From here, you can only go up. But do not try to move too far, too fast. You could defeat the whole object if you put too much strain on an out-of-condition system. Make up your mind to get your problems sorted out. You have started working on it: do not let anything stop you!

Cardiovascular signs and symptoms

You may suspect that you have already experienced symptoms of cardiovascular disease, but have not consulted a doctor about them. This section is intended to clarify the question.

Self-assessment on the basis of a short questionnaire is not likely to produce a very reliable guide to the presence or absence of cardiovascular symptoms; there are too many sources of confusion, and when you are not face-to-face with somebody who has expertise in the area, such confusion cannot be sorted out. If you finish this questionnaire convinced that you have had half a dozen heart attacks already, bear in mind that it could have been indigestion. If you are inclined to dash to your doctor to announce that you are close to death from heart disease, on the basis of this chapter, pause and read the first few pages of *Three Men in a Boat* first! However, if you are concerned that your heart may already be showing signs of damage, by all means consult a doctor to check up.

It may be necessary to pace yourself very carefully when you work towards improved health. It would be foolish to precipitate a heart attack in your efforts to avoid having one, and if you have been having symptoms of heart disease, you run a much higher risk of catastrophic breakdown.

Chest Pain on Effort

Have you ever had any pain or discomfort in your chest?
    If Yes:
Do you get it when you walk uphill or hurry?
    If No, the pain is not likely to be due to heart disease.
Do you get pain in your left arm, shoulder or jaw when you walk uphill or hurry?
    If Yes, this could possibly be 'reflected' chest pain – chest pain felt elsewhere in the body. Continue.
What do you do if you get chest pain while walking?
    If you can carry on (without taking nitroglycerine), the pain is not likely to be due to heart disease.
If you stand still, what happens to the pain?
    If the pain is relieved in less than 10 minutes, it could be angina. Angina is equally common in men and women, but it is a very much more serious symptom in men.
Have you ever had a very severe pain across the front of your chest which lasted for half an hour or more?
    If Yes, this might possibly have been a heart attack. These do occur without producing dramatic symptoms that necessitate medical attention. If you think it has happened to you fairly recently, you would be wise to have your suspicions checked by a doctor. Characteristic changes in the pattern of electrical activity of the heart are capable of revealing any damage to the heart muscle.

Hyperventilation

Hyperventilation is very common among cardiac patients. It is a breathing pattern which can cause serious heart symptoms. Although rarely recognised, and not mentioned in most medical textbooks, it was described as long ago as 1871. It has been called 'irritable heart', 'effort syndrome' and 'hyperventilation syndrome'. All those who experience any symptoms that could be due to heart disease should check the possibility that they are suffering from hyperventilation. Fortunately, it can be controlled readily by the sufferer and an immediate and dramatic improvement usually follows understanding.

The most common sign of this syndrome is probably the feeling that you cannot get quite enough air. Sufferers often breathe irregularly, with deep sighs at intervals and frequent throat-clearing as they struggle for more breath. Paradoxically, the problem is that they actually breathe too much, but rather shallowly.

Check the following symptoms. You may suffer from some, though probably not all of them.

Chronic tiredness and lack of stamina; weakness; disturbed sleep; headache; excessive sweating; sensations of feeling cold; poor concentration and performance.

Numbness and tingling of the extremities; giddiness; blurred or tunnel vision; fainting.

Sensation of breathlessness or inability to take a deep enough breath; yawning; non-productive cough; night-time breathing problems.

Chest pains; angina; palpitations; fast heart rate.

Belching; abdominal bloating; heartburn; sensation of lump in throat; dry mouth.

Muscle tightness, stiffness, and cramps.

Anxiety; sensation of being far away from yourself; fears; depression; panic attacks.

These are very common symptoms and most can have causes other than hyperventilation. You can check whether hyperventilating is the cause by deliberately doing it.

First, equip yourself with a paper bag, about 6" by 10". Sit in a comfortable chair in front of a clock or large watch and practise breathing at a rate of 30 to 40 deep breaths per minute. When you are familiar with this breathing rate, make yourself breathe in this way for up to five minutes.

You can expect to feel light-headed and tired, and your mouth will probably go dry. You may also recognise some of the other symptoms you have been experiencing.

After five minutes, or when your symptoms have established themselves, hold the paper bag over your mouth and nose and use it to re-breathe your expired air. After a fairly short period of breathing from the bag, your symptoms will disappear again.

If you found that this provocation test did indeed bring on your symptoms, you now also know how to stop them. Make sure that you have access to a paper bag and use it to re-breathe your expired air as soon as symptoms begin.

Leg Pain

1 Do you get pain in either leg when walking?
2 Does this pain ever begin when you are standing still or sitting?
3 Do you feel the pain in your calf or calves?
4 Does the pain begin most rapidly if you walk uphill or hurry?
5 Does the pain ever disappear if you continue walking?
6 Does the pain disappear within 10 minutes if you stop walking?

If you answered Yes to questions 1, 3, 4 and 6, and a definite No to questions 2 and 5, the pain could be due to intermittent claudication, the most common symptom of inadequate blood supply to the muscles of the legs. It usually means that there are large deposits of cholesterol in the arteries feeding the legs and feet. Radical change, in diet and activity patterns, can often undo much of the damage.

CHAPTER 4

Does Medicine Have the Answer?

All professions are conspiracies against the laity
George Bernard Shaw *The Doctor's Dilemma*

In this chapter we will be looking at the main areas of conventional medical treatment for cardiovascular disease. We will start by considering drug therapy, since this is the treatment offered to most people. Detailed information on particular drugs is given in chapter 9 under the headings emphasised in the text.

Drugs are the primary therapy for most illnesses. Each person in Britain has on average six prescriptions from their general practitioner each year, and although it has been estimated that three quarters of all consultations arise from non-medical problems, eighty per cent of consultations end with pre-scriptions for drugs.

Drugs prescribed by general practitioners for cardiovascular problems cost the NHS £300 million in 1982, and the figure rises with every year. Recently, there has been a boom in drug development and prescribing for heart disease. Between 1970 and 1982, the use of heart preparations (mainly beta-blockers) rose by 325 per cent, diuretics (water tablets) by 205 per cent.

Overall, products for cardiovascular disease now account for about a quarter of the total NHS drug bill.

A general rule applies to all drug therapy. All but a few drugs suppress symptoms, they are not cures. It is much safer, and in the long term much more effective, to cope with illness by dealing with its causes. Suppressing symptoms with drugs while you carry on living in the way that developed the illness is a recipe for disaster.

Drug treatment for heart problems has a very long history, one which has been well documented since the publication in 1785 of *Account of the Foxglove*, written by the Shropshire doctor William Withering. The foxglove was used by wise women of the countryside to treat dropsy, the accumulation of water in the body which follows heart problems. It is still used for the same purpose today, though rather than drink a tea brewed from the leaves of the plant, people take digitalis or digoxin (foxglove extract) in tablet form. Dr Withering quickly discovered the problem of all use of powerful drugs, whether they be 'natural herbs' or synthetic products, for the treatment of disease. Foxglove can be valuable, but also very dangerous, a potent poison. If a patient took too much, or proved unusually sensitive to a normal dose, the consequences could be fatal.

Although few drugs in common use are as poisonous as foxglove leaves and their extracts, the unpalatable fact is that all drugs are dangerous. There is no such thing as a totally safe drug in conventional medicine. No amount of testing is likely to produce such a thing. It is not that drug manufacturers behave irresponsibly in unleashing poisonous products on the market (although some have). The problem lies in the way drugs work. Basically, their effects are more general than they would ideally be; they affect the whole body, not just the heart or whatever organ or process they are intended to affect. Drug use, therefore, is always a delicate balance of potential value against potential risk.

But we like taking medicines. In many ways our society is addicted to the idea. Swallowing a pill, or even nasty medicine, makes us feel good, irrespective of the actual effect. For doctors it offers an apparently easy way to practise medicine. For drug manufacturers it is such a good business proposition that they have been dubbed the 'no recession' industry.

Against this background we should not be surprised that doctors offering alternatives to drugs are a rarity. Although many are worried by the dominance of their profession's reliance on pharmaceuticals, they find it hard to break the habit. The delicacy of judgement required is frequently lacking, and the hope of benefit tends to outweigh caution all too often. With every increase in the use of prescription drugs, there is a rise in the rate of occurrence of drug-induced disease. Preparations for cardiovascular disease are among the commonest causes of such illness. The number of deaths due to treatment is not known; what is certain is that it is much higher than estimated, and far higher than it need be.

Ironically, supposed absence of side-effects is now the most popular selling-point in advertising campaigns for new drugs for heart disease. Experience shows that such claims should not be accepted at face value. As we write this book, yet another heart drug, advertised as having 'a wide safety margin' and of which the manufacturers said 'side-effects seem minimal', has been the subject of a warning. This was issued by the government 'watchdog', the Committee on Safety of Medicines, after it was informed of the deaths of seven patients and severe reactions in more than a hundred. The drug is Cordarone X. It is used to treat disturbances of heart rhythm. This is just one of a continuing series of drugs launched as safe which prove, in practice, to be very dangerous. Eraldin, a beta-blocker, was withdrawn in 1975 after around seven thousand people had suffered irreversible injury and some had died. It, too, was claimed to be particularly safe.

Heavy promotion through advertising in medical journals, through the media and through 'conferences' supported by the manufacturers with invited pro-drug speakers push home the message that the answer to every malfunction is a drug. Indeed, it is frequently implied that only drug therapy is effective, and that any doctor who fails to prescribe drugs for patients with cardiovascular symptoms is putting their lives at risk.

Whenever a doctor initiates a course of treatment, there is unavoidable uncertainty. It covers many areas; uncertainty about the individual patient's reaction to therapy, uncertainty about the effects of the preparations in the long term, uncertainty about the natural history of the disease in that person. At the same time, the doctor feels obliged to do something: to offer some sort of therapy that will get rid of this patient's symptoms. Under these circumstances it is imperative that both doctor and patient have access to unbiased information on every possible aspect of the problem, and that the doctor particularly pays close attention to such information.

Regrettably, these conditions are not fulfilled. Doctors' training and the information they are given about drug therapy are systematically biased. They are led to believe that drugs are more effective than they actually are, and that their dangers are usually negligible. The result is a general tendency to over-prescribe drugs of all sorts.

Part of the reason for this lies in the methods used in medicine to judge the effectiveness of therapy. Clinical trials are used to show that a particular form of treatment is superior to another, or to no treatment at all. Unfortunately, these trials are carried out under conditions which simply do not hold in the real world. Outside the rarefied air of the clinical trial, patients are not selected with the same care, and their condition is not monitored in the same way. The result is that problems are not observed and dealt with as quickly and efficiently.

To make matters worse, clinical trials are subtly biased in their design. With rare exceptions, a drug is compared with a placebo, a neutral substance which is assumed to be as near nothing as one can get. We have yet to see a clinical trial which includes a comparison group which receives any of the available non-drug therapies, or modifies smoking, eating, activity and relaxation patterns. This sort of integrated non-drug approach has never been proved less effective than drugs or surgery, despite the fact that its undoubted safety and rationality should make it the first choice of treatment.

There is a considerable body of research showing that treatment is often given when it is neither necessary nor appropriate. Such treatment is inevitably hazardous, and the risk is not balanced by benefit. Bias in favour of treatment is general throughout medicine. Doctors want to do what they were trained for, often to excess.

This has given rise to the 'doctor anomaly': which is that over a certain minimum level more doctors in a population means more illness and more deaths. Overprescribing of drugs for cardiovascular problems is well documented. Among the elderly especially, the hazards of drugs are likely to outweigh their benefits. Study after study has revealed that many old people can cease to take their medication, and feel the better as a result.

The problem for anyone who is taking one or more of these preparations is to decide whether they are appropriate, whether they are causing other symptoms and whether it would be wiser to continue to take them or to tail them off. Our general advice to such people is that they should do all they can to improve their condition by making the sort of lifestyle changes that we recommend in this book. Most should be able to wean themselves off drugs with their doctors' agreement. After all, if you are taking tablets for blood pressure and you succeed in reducing your blood pressure to a level below which your doctor thinks you should take tablets, then you get off the drugs and improve your chances of avoiding more serious symptoms.

We must emphasise that we do not believe that all those who are taking drugs for cardiovascular disease should immediately give up taking their tablets. But we hope that they will be able to progress to a state of health where drugs are unnecessary, and that those who treat them will encourage them in this endeavour.

The next section of this chapter will deal generally with the types of drugs used in rough order of importance. This list cannot be completely comprehensive because the range is growing all the time, and new brand names are being added every month. Most of these are broadly the same as their predecessors, so if you are unable to find information about the tablets you take, try to find out what type of drug they contain. Your pharmacist will often be willing to help. Then consult a more detailed source for further information if necessary. Details of suitable sources are listed in chapter 9.

The majority of people whose doctors decide they should be treated for cardiovascular symptoms today will be given *beta-blockers* (p. 218). These are perhaps the most 'successful' group of drugs in recent years. Where once tranquillisers were recommended for everything, their virtues unquestioned and their hazards apparently nonexistent, beta-blockers are now paramount.

Beta-blockers are prescribed for a whole spectrum of heart problems. They are the drugs of first choice for high blood pressure, angina and disturbances of heart rhythm; they are used to protect heart attack victims from another attack, to slow the heart-rate and to reduce anxiety. They are prescribed for disorders ranging from migraine to thyroid abnormalities. These are the best-selling drugs of the 1980s in every developed country where heart disease is a problem.

Beta-blockers may reduce high blood pressure and the symptoms of angina. So popular have they become that about one adult in fifteen in Britain is now regularly taking them. Two assumptions about beta-blockade support this very high level of use of the drugs: one is that they are effective; the second is that they are a safe way of dealing with symptoms.

The short-term effectiveness cannot be doubted. Angina sufferers, particularly, are well aware of their benefits. However, they have not had any detectable impact on the heart disease death-rate. In the United States, where the decline in coronary deaths has been most marked, beta-blockade did not become widespread until well after the death-rate had already begun to fall. In Britain, the fluctuations in death-rates show no relation to beta-blocker use. Indeed, in the one year when the steady rise in acceptance of beta-blockade was reversed because of fears about their safety (1975), the death-rate fell more than it had in the previous or succeeding years. And in Sweden, where beta-blockers have figured consistently in the Top Ten prescription drugs for some years, the death-rate shows no sign of declining.

Judging from this data, we are bound to conclude that the main benefits of beta-blockade are in the subjective experience of those who take them. Angina sufferers, especially, may be grateful that beta-blockade is available. However, some find that it makes their symptoms worse. And what of the many thousands who do not actually feel better for taking the tablets? Are they receiving appropriate therapy – or could the assumed benefits be less than the risk of using these potent drugs?

Dr Peter Nixon, an eminent consultant cardiologist, who has been observing the effects of the rising popularity of beta-blockade, is profoundly disturbed by it. In an editorial in the *American Heart Journal* (August, 1980), he wrote that, 'Iatrogenic disorder ... has been expanded beyond belief by the beta-blockers. It is now commonplace to encounter the expected and reversible complications of reduced cardiac output such as cerebral vascular insufficiency, intermittent claudication, weakness, tiredness and inability to cope with tasks; and a frequent cause of consultation is the patient's inability to convince his doctor that the beta-blocker is doing nothing to halt his deterioration towards a second or third myocardial infarction. In some cases the doctor thought the drug effects were caused by arteriosclerotic deterioration. In other cases he has recognised the noxious effects of his therapy but the propaganda has made him fear to stop it. All too often the doctor was so persuaded of the drug's virtues that he closed his mind to his patients' heretical reports.'

Dr Nixon goes on to explain in detail why he believes that beta-blockers may make matters worse for cardiac patients.

Basically, it comes down to the fact that no beta-blocker could ever damp down the effects of arousal or exercise throughout the system, because they act only on parts of it. And by blocking warning signs, they allow people to continue to subject themselves to levels of strain that exceed their capacity. The underlying point is that it may not be wise to suppress a symptom like angina, however unpleasant it may be. The pain has a message. If the angina patient wishes to recover and return to full health, then this message must be listened to and acted on.

The second general problem with the use of beta-blockers, or any other drug which alters physiological responses, is that the body will try to adapt in such a way as to cancel the drug effects. This means that the drug will gradually become less effective as time goes on. Beta-blockers are taken for an indefinite period. Doctors normally assume that a drug prescribed for high blood pressure will have to be prescribed for the rest of the patient's life. That could mean many decades. During this time, its benefits will tend to disappear. They will be matched by an equal and opposite reaction from hormone systems as the brain tries to return the body to a state which suits the pressures to which the person is exposed. If high blood pressure develops in response to environmental stresses, then it must be considered 'adaptive'. As far as the mid-brain (the central control mechanism which determines blood pressure) is concerned, high blood pressure is a desirable state. So it will raise blood pressure by an assortment of hormonal adaptations.

The result is stepwise therapy. The patient who starts out by taking beta-blockers (for life) will in due course have to take another drug (again for life); and when the two drugs eventually fail to reduce blood pressure to the level the doctor believes appropriate, then another will be added. And perhaps another. Or alternatively another more potent, but also more dangerous, drug will have to be substituted for the now-impotent cocktail that the patient is taking.

This process can only end in disease or disaster. The causes of the stress that the body is reacting to by producing symptoms are still at work. In addition, the body is increasingly stressed by measures designed to suppress those symptoms. And the body is constantly having to deal with artificial substances which put a strain on its de-toxifying systems. It is struggling to overcome the effects of these substances while maintaining the delicate biochemical balance that supports life. While the heart might perhaps benefit from all this drug therapy, other organs and tissues will undoubtedly suffer.

The form of this suffering will depend on the individual. It is a matter of biochemistry and individual vulnerability. Some drug reactions are described as 'idiosyncratic', a term which reflects the unpredictability of the more serious illnesses caused by drugs. Some doctors will find fault with this analysis. They would suggest that they would recognise drug-induced disease more often if it were as common and as inevitable as we contend. Regrettably, it has been found on many occasions that doctors tend not to see drug-induced illness, even when it is staring them in the face. They are not objective observers of the effects of the therapies they use. Most will assume symptoms are of natural origin, and will fail to question the drugs. This is a major problem, which we describe in detail in our book *Cured to Death*.

Sometimes it is impossible to deny the reality of drug-induced disease. With one early beta-blocker, practolol (Eraldin), the damage was so strange, so unpleasant and so widespread that the drug had to be withdrawn from general use. When the hazards of practolol became generally known, doctors and patients were faced with the problem of withdrawal from beta-blockers. Withdrawal from all anxiety-reducing drugs, from tranquillisers and sleeping pills to heroin, can be dangerous and unpleasant. This danger means that people taking beta-blockers are caught in a cleft stick. They may dislike the effects of the drug, but they fear to stop it.

We would reassure readers who are in this position that they can withdraw from these drugs.

It would be foolish to gamble, as some practolol victims did, by stopping dead and risking rebound disturbances of heart rhythm which could precipitate heart attack. But if withdrawal is done gradually, when the individual is well rested and has arranged to avoid situations which produce high levels of arousal, it can be quite safe. Dr Nixon routinely stops beta-blockade in his patients as part of their preparation for cardiac conditioning training in a gymnasium.

The potential ill-effects of beta-blockers are many, though some people taking them feel perfectly normal. Effects and adverse reactions affect many body systems and include excessively low blood pressure, fainting and a reduced blood supply to the extremities, which results in cold hands and feet and a worsening of leg pain due to intermittent claudication.

A group of hospitals centred on Boston, Massachusetts, has been collaborating since 1966 in the surveillance of adverse effects of drugs in hospital patients. They reported that about two per cent of patients experience 'life-threatening' adverse reactions to beta-blockers. These reactions generally occur with low doses, early in therapy. The most important are unwanted effects on the cardiovascular system.

Obviously, hospital patients are a special group. They are already sicker than most of the people who are given prescriptions for beta-blockers by their general practitioners. They are likely to be taking a range of other drugs when they are put on beta-blockers, and the more drugs a person takes, the higher are the chances of adverse reactions. So it would be quite wrong to extrapolate from these figures, to propose that one person in fifty risks death from the effects of the first few beta-blockers he or she takes. But we must be aware that the hazards that show up in hospital patients are the hazards of the drugs themselves. The level of risk varies with the susceptibility of the individual – and nobody knows for sure how sensitive he or she may be to the effects of beta-blockade.

For all that, there are circumstances where the potential benefits of beta-blockade will outweigh the risks. The essential point is that these drugs should never be taken casually. They are powerful drugs which must be treated with the greatest respect. It is possible to avoid them, by taking appropriate steps to deal with symptoms by non-drug means, and you can be sure that your general health will be better.

Diuretics (p. 219) are prescribed for heart patients as often as beta-blockers. The rationale that underlies their use is that by stimulating urination, they reduce blood volume and hence reduce blood pressure. People with cardiac problems frequently suffer from puffy ankles, a commonplace sign of water retention; some may also be breathless because of excessive fluid accumulation in the lungs. Diuretics offer effective treatment for these problems.

Among the elderly, diuretic use is very common indeed. One recent survey of people over seventy years of age revealed that one in three were taking diuretics. Other studies have shown that more than half of these patients can be taken off diuretics with no ill-effects.

Water retention is caused by a hormone action that encourages the kidneys to reabsorb sodium and water from the urine. Diuretics generally induce increased excretion of salts, usually both sodium and potassium. Water is excreted at the same time because the kidney works by matching the concentrations of salts in the urine and the blood flowing through its tubules. If a drug makes the urine more concentrated, water will be drawn from the blood to dilute it. Hence the final effect is a reduction in blood volume.

Interfering with this delicate balance has unwelcome consequences. If the dose of diuretic is low and the person is not sensitive to its hazards, then there may be no problems with years of treatment. This happy situation is not experienced by everyone.

The best recognised hazard of diuretic treatment is accelerated excretion of potassium. We saw earlier that the sodium/potassium salt balance is already widely disrupted in our culture. Further loss of potassium can be a serious problem because it leads to disturbances of heart-beat. The greatest danger occurs in people who are also taking drugs like digoxin (see *cardiac glycosides*, below), as potassium deficiency enhances their hazards.

There are three ways of getting round the potassium problem. One is to take the diuretic on alternate days, and to have periods free from diuretic use when potassium levels can build up. This can be an adequate safeguard for those whose diet is high in potassium. But discuss this with your doctor before you do it. Anyone taking diuretics should make sure they eat plenty of raw or dried fruit and lots of fresh vegetables.

Second, potassium supplements may be given, often in the same tablet. In the list of diuretics in chapter 9 (p. 219), some products have the letter K at the end of the brand name. K is the chemical symbol for potassium, which is in combination with a diuretic. Others may be in supplement form. Unfortunately, giving potassium supplements can cause problems too. The side-effects of these products include nausea, vomiting and ulceration of the oesophagus or gut. A liquid preparation of potassium chloride is the safest, such as Kay-Cee-L Elixir.

The third option involves the use of a different type of diuretic, one which does not deplete the body's potassium. These *potassium-sparing diuretics* (p. 219) are not normally the drugs of first choice, mainly because they are rather weak and they have markedly less impact on blood pressure. They are also expensive. Potassium-sparing diuretics are marked * in the list.

The problem of ineffectiveness can be overcome while maintaining a satisfactory potassium level by the use of two types of diuretic simultaneously. Not ones to miss an opportunity for a competitive edge in marketing, the drug companies have once again produced *combination products* which contain both types of drug in the same tablet. These are marked thus: # in the list.

Caution: If you are taking any potassium-sparing diuretic, whether on its own or in combination with another diuretic, you should not take any form of potassium supplement. The risk is of potassium overdose. High levels of potassium in the body induced by the use of potassium-sparing diuretics can and do cause deaths. The danger is greater if you take potassium supplements.

Problems with potassium are not the only adverse effects of diuretics. Although they are relatively safe, most set off well-recognised metabolic effects which will tend to make the heart disease problem worse for some of the patients who take them. One is hyperglycaemia, or a raised blood sugar level. Here we encounter the diabetes problem once more.

Not only do the most commonly used diuretics make diabetes more severe, but they also precipitate diabetes in some people. It is believed by doctors that diuretics only cause diabetes in people who are already prone to the condition; however, we fail to see how it is possible to discriminate between these individuals and others until they develop the symptoms of diabetes. How often the use of diuretics causes diabetes is not known. Many of those who take diuretics could be expected to become diabetic even if they did not take the drugs. The diabetes looks the same whatever its cause. So doctors will tend to assume that it would have developed anyway.

The situation with gout is similar. Diuretics are known to be capable of precipitating gout, but many patients who develop this painful condition while taking diuretics have no idea that there could be a connection.

The next group of drugs used are the *antihypertensives*. This group contains *vasodilators* (p.221), *centrally acting antihypertensives* (p. 221), *adrenergic nerve blockers* (p. 222), *alpha blocking drugs* (p. 222) and *enzyme inhibitors* (p. 223). These drugs have a variety of actions, but all are aimed at reducing blood pressure.

Antihypertensives are not normally drugs of first choice for the reduction of blood pressure. They are usually used in addition to beta-blockers and diuretics, when these two safer drugs together are incapable of reducing blood pressure to the level desired by the doctor. Adverse reactions are not uncommon, and they are made all the more probable by the simultaneous use of other potent drugs.

Vasodilators reduce blood pressure by increasing the bore of blood vessels. All the arteries of the body, from the largest to the smallest, have muscular walls and are capable of expanding or contracting according to need. If there is generalised expansion throughout the body, blood pressure falls. This can occur very fast indeed under natural conditions, for example in shock after an accident.

The existence of this natural rapid-action system of blood pressure control makes it an inevitable target for drug treatment. The danger is that the effect of therapy on blood pressure can be excessive. Great caution is essential in the use of such products. Despite this, vasodilators are now preferred for antihypertensive therapy over drugs which were used in the 1960s and 1970s because the problems associated with the use of these previously popular drugs may be even greater. These were the centrally acting antihypertensives, particularly methyldopa.

Unfortunately, the systems on which methyldopa acts have many diverse links with other body systems. Consequently, the range of adverse effects which have been attributed to methyldopa is enormous. This drug can cause a variety of blood problems, but the most common is destruction of the red blood cells, leading to anaemia. Another reaction can complicate therapy by making transfusion hazardous. This develops in twenty per cent of people taking methyldopa. The Boston Collaborative study found that methyldopa had an 18.4 per cent adverse reaction rate and a 19 per cent failure rate in hospital patients.

One of the most common reactions to methyldopa in men is impotence. Only seven per cent of men spontaneously complain of this embarrassing effect, but over half are likely to suffer from it. Serious liver damage has also been attributed to methyldopa. This can take a variety of forms, some of which may be fatal. Jaundice, the first symptom of liver malfunction, may appear between three and sixteen weeks after therapy begins. The drug must be withdrawn immediately if this happens.

Another drug in this class is clonidine hydrochloride. This

seems to work by interfering with the signals from the brain which would raise blood pressure. Effectively, its action is to reduce arousal. When this goes further than desired, the drug is said to cause drowsiness, but this cannot be regarded as a side-effect. It is merely an extension of the therapeutic effect.

Our final drug in this class was the first antihypertensive to be discovered. In the 1950s, reserpine and related alkaloids were the only drugs available for the treatment of high blood pressure, and they were widely used. They have since fallen from favour for two reasons. First, they are no longer profitable. Second, they can induce such deep depression that they may even precipitate suicide. Other adverse effects are broadly similar to clonidine hydrochloride, with the addition of one serious long-term risk – an increased susceptibility to breast cancer among women.

Today, the main use of reserpine is in research. It blocks one of the major chemical systems in the brain which controls the transmission of nerve impulses concerned with arousal and mood, and is used to produce experimental animals in whom this system does not function. These creatures, of course, are given higher doses of reserpine than people would be likely to receive, but sensitivity varies between individuals of any species. Nobody who has ever come face to face with a reserpised cat, observed its misery, seen its fur matted with vomit and heard its desperate cries, would be able to forget the horrible effects that this drug can produce in the hands of scientists.

Adrenergic nerve blockers tend to reduce blood pressure when a person is standing up. They act by blocking the effects of nerves which cause constriction of the arteries, that inner girding of loins. They have fallen out of favour because they produce faintness on rising, and are not effective when the patient is lying down. Their side-effects are not dramatic.

Alpha-blocking drugs are normally given at the same time as beta-blockers. They are used to control high blood pressure which resists treatment by beta-blockade and diuretics. Like the drugs above, they block the effects of adrenergic nerves. In the case of this group, the block is at the point of nerve input. Since they affect the same system as the centrally-acting antihypertensives, they have many of the same disadvantages.

The enzyme inhibitors (p. 223) are the newest development in drugs aimed at controlling high blood pressure. Captopril acts by interfering with angiotensin, one of the hormones which raises blood pressure, by preventing its conversion into an active form. Captopril is appropriately used only as a last resort for severe hypertension. It is a particularly dangerous drug. Paradoxically, captopril therapy may seem less unpleasant for the patient than taking a safer drug, so it may be more readily accepted.

As we write this book, the manufacturers of Capoten (Squibb) are running an advertising campaign aimed at doctors which emphasises the acceptability of the product. Doctors are concerned about the unpleasantness of treatment for high blood pressure. Patients who feel perfectly well untreated, as most people with high blood pressure do, are naturally reluctant to take pills indefinitely that make them feel ill. So the advertising line (taken from a prestigious medical journal article) that goes, 'For the first time ever a patient can feel as well on treatment for high blood pressure as he does off it', is likely to persuade doctors to prescribe Capoten (the brand name). This, of course, is precisely the intention of the advertisement.

The small print in the bottom left hand corner of the advertisement contains the instructions on the use of this drug, the warnings and the details of those side-effects admitted by the company. This information should make doctors very wary of the product. Unfortunately for their patients' safety, the words are so tiny that they produce what looks like a grey block. The most important warnings concern the effects on the bone marrow. Captopril can depress the production of white blood cells and interfere with immunity. This means that even minor infections could be dangerous, as susceptibility to infection is much increased. According to the small print, 'All patients treated with Capoten should be told to report any signs of infection (eg sore throat, fever). A complete white blood cell count should be done immediately when such a report is made.' White blood cell counts should be done regularly when captopril is taken by anyone with possible kidney problems or connective tissue disease.

Caution: Captopril tends to raise body potassium levels, so it should not be taken at the same time as potassium supplements or potassium-sparing diuretics. Other potentially serious adverse reactions to captopril include skin rashes, which can be severe and long-lasting, and kidney damage. In addition, it may cause loss of taste, inflammation of the inside of the mouth, abdominal pain and dizziness.

The next group of drugs are the *cardiac glycosides* (p. 223), the modern descendants of William Withering's dried foxglove leaves. Although effective treatments for heart failure, cardiac glycosides have serious drawbacks. Basically, the problem with these drugs is this: the difference between a therapeutic dose and a dose that will cause poisoning is very small, and it varies with the individual. Intoxication by cardiac glycosides is common among the people who take them, and deaths are not infrequent. The problem is particularly acute among the elderly, whose bodies are less able to break down and eliminate drugs. It is in this population who are most likely to be given such drugs that the proportion of toxic reactions is highest.

One report on maintenance therapy with digoxin revealed that 27 of the 80 elderly patients studied suffered toxic effects. Treatment was withdrawn from 59 of the patients in the group, with no ill-effects. It was concluded that digoxin might be withdrawn from all elderly patients except those with seriously damaged hearts.

Another type of *vasodilator* (p. 224) is also used for angina. Some people will be familiar with its effects even if they have never experienced angina. Many of these vasodilators are essentially the same as 'poppers', popular 'recreational drugs'. It is said that they heighten sexual arousal, though our experience is that the rapid heart-beat and headache that can be produced in healthy people in no way enhances any pleasure. Beware ancient hippies bearing vials of amyl nitrite!

The drugs in this group are available in a wide variety of forms, including a patch designed to stick to the skin of the sufferer's chest, ointments, chewable tablets, capsules, sprays to be used under the tongue and solutions for injection. Their main effect is dilation of veins. Blood pools in the peripheral veins, reducing the quantity of blood returning to the heart and thus reducing its workload. With less blood to pump, the heart needs less oxygen, but it may actually receive more, because these drugs also dilate the coronary arteries. The net effect is relief from the pain of angina.

People who frequently suffer from angina may prevent the onset of attacks by sucking a short-acting nitrate tablet just before doing anything they think may bring on an attack. Short-acting nitrates can also be used to cut short an angina attack, and have been used in this way for over a hundred years. These are the tablets for which the stricken middle-aged hero gasps desperately in many 'B' movies, sucking the tablets found just in time by the beautiful caring female lead. The hero revives, returning regularly from death's door. In reality, he is unlikely to have died without them; this is a part of the myth creation that has shaped our beliefs about the power of drugs.

The danger they pose is that, although these drugs may be safe in themselves, they allow the overstressing of the heart to continue. With the relief of symptoms, the problem is assumed to have been solved and the patient may ignore the need to avoid pain-producing stress.

Most of the drugs in this group are remarkably safe for occasional use, although unwanted effects such as flushing, headache, dizziness and faintness on rising may limit their value. The hazards are greater for the longer-acting preparations which are taken regularly, but even these usually cause no more severe side-effects than swollen ankles.

Other preparations are designed to be taken regularly to prevent angina. We have dealt with the most important of these products, the beta-blockers, earlier in this chapter. Many angina patients take both beta-blockers and vasodilating drugs.

Calcium antagonists (p. 224) are rather different from other vasodilators. Their primary effect, the dilation of blood vessels feeding the heart and tissues, is the same as that of the nitrates. The calcium antagonists are gaining ground steadily in therapy for heart disease, and we expect to see a proliferation of drugs of this type over the next few years.

Calcium is crucially involved in the contraction of muscle cells in many parts of the cardiovascular system. Calcium antagonists, by interfering with this process, tend to reduce the force of contraction of the heart muscle. But this is balanced by the reduction of workload that results from vasodilation. Side-effects of these drugs are generally similar to those of other vasodilators.

Peripheral vasodilators (p. 225), frequently prescribed for diseased vessels feeding the limbs, are introduced by the authoritative *British National Formulary (BNF)* with this comment: 'Most serious peripheral disorders are now known to be due to occlusions of vessels; ... use of vasodilators may increase blood flow at rest, but no controlled studies have shown any improvement in walking distance or sustained increase in muscle blood flow during exercise. Rest pain is rarely affected.' We interpret this as meaning that these drugs are useless to relieve pain under any circumstances. There seems to be no justification for taking them. Fortunately, ceasing to take them is not known to cause any new problems.

Cerebral vasodilators (p. 225) get shorter treatment by the *BNF* in its academic fashion: 'These drugs are claimed to improve mental function ... (they) have not been shown clinically to be of much benefit in senile dementia.' The rationale that underlies their use is that improvement in blood flow in the brain will reverse some of the effects of damage to the blood supply by the small strokes which can cause progressive deterioration in mental function. As with the peripheral vasodilators, they may do no good at all but they can still produce side-effects.

Anticoagulants (p. 225) interfere with the blood's ability to clot. They are appropriately used when there is a high risk of development of blood clots in vessels, which may then cause blockage. They are most valuable for people who have undergone heart valve surgery; if clots come to rest in the artificial valve, the result can be death. Blood clotting is another finely balanced process. If the dose of anticoagulant is slightly too high, the result is bleeding into the tissues of the body. If the blood coagulates too readily, the result may be deep-vein thrombosis, or clots in the veins. So anyone on anticoagulants needs constant monitoring, to check the length of time the blood takes to clot.

Haemorrhage is the main adverse effect of anticoagulant therapy. Minor bleeding shows up as spontaneous bruising, black faeces or blood in the urine. Massive bleeding into the abdomen or muscles requires transfusion and injections of vitamin K – the vitamin that is antagonised by these drugs. Cerebral haemorrhage is often fatal. Anyone who needs to take anticoagulants should carry a warning card. These should be available from doctors or hospital pharmacies.

The chance of giving birth to a malformed baby is increased by anticoagulant therapy, and it should be avoided in the first three months of pregnancy. It should also be avoided in the weeks before the baby is expected since it can lead to haemorrhage in both mother and child.

Drugs which reduce blood cholesterol (p. 226) are now considered appropriate for only a minority of people, those with abnormally high blood cholesterol levels. They are effective in reducing cholesterol, but the problems with therapy outweigh its benefits for most people.

One of these drugs, clofibrate (Atromid S), was the subject of a massive trial organised by the World Health Organisation; 15,745 volunteers participated, accumulating between them 83,534 treatment years of experience with the drug. Atromid S was selling very well after early reports suggested that it was capable of reducing heart attacks in a large proportion of the susceptible population, so it was considered essential that its role in therapy should be clearly defined.

The results proved intensely disturbing both for the manufacturers of the drug and the medical profession. For it was found that the death-rate in the group of people taking the drug was significantly higher than that in the untreated group. And while clofibrate reduced the incidence of non-fatal heart attacks, it did not affect the number of deaths due to heart attack.

The clofibrate trial represents a milestone in objective assessment of drug therapy. For the first time, it forced the medical profession to recognise that a drug was capable of producing non-specific hazards. The increased death-rate in the group taking clofibrate did not result from any clearly defined group of causes; the drug seemed to have a rather general effect which some people have attributed to accelerated aging. It is the sort of problem which would never be picked up in general use. It also must raise far-reaching doubts about the wisdom of metabolic interference by the rather crude means that drug therapy represents.

One might be forgiven for concluding that with so many sorts of drugs for so many purposes (and usually dozens of different brands of near-identical drugs available in each class), consumed by millions each year, at enormous cost to the community, heart disease would be in retreat. Far from it. They appear to have little positive benefit at all. Indeed, if you consider the known hazards, and what could be done with the resources they represent, drugs may be part of the problem rather than part of the answer.

Doctors must be aware that their first line therapy is not stopping the heart disease epidemic. In view of this one might expect some pause, some consideration that perhaps conventional medicine might have got it wrong. There is only a minimal sign of this, and other therapeutic directions are, as we noted, rare. The result of the current strategy amounts to an exercise in hope while things get worse. The next step is to offer surgery as an answer.

Many people see coronary bypass as one of the wonders of our age. Patients who were crippled by angina go through a bypass operation and come out free from symptoms. In Britain, the number of bypass operations carried out rose to over 6,000 per year by 1984. Surgeons would do many more if the resources were available to them; 25,000 a year is the target for many cardiologists, although, according to a leading article in the *British Medical Journal*, bypass should not be considered unless the patient is incapable of climbing a single flight of stairs without pain. If this criterion were generally adopted, the number of operations would fall precipitously.

The technique of bypass surgery is nearly twenty years old. During that time, some teams of surgeons and supportive staff have developed skills of formidable refinement, and the results they can achieve are reported to be excellent. However, all forms of intervention at this level of sophistication are heavily dependent on the knowledge, abilities and facilities available to the team carrying out the operation. The benefits and risks of coronary bypass vary greatly from place to place, from team to team; and it is inevitably true that the most publicised groups are the most successful. If the Mayo Clinic of America carries out a series of bypass operations with demonstrably excellent results, its success is likely to be reported in widely-read medical journals.

Less favoured groups may pick up the method, and assume that they are capable of emulating the leaders in the field. Unfortunately, this belief is often unwarranted. The benefits shown by surgery carried out by one team will not be shared by the efforts of most others. So people whose views about the efficacy of surgery are formed on the basis of published results of trials of the method will tend to have overly favourable impressions. This is another part of the general problem of assessment of medical measures.

Coronary bypass had already been used more widely than any other form of surgical intervention for heart disease by 1974. It involves the replacement of damaged and occluded coronary arteries with pieces of vein taken from the patient's leg. Through these new vessels, the heart muscle gets sufficient blood to meet its needs, and the result can be dramatic relief from angina.

Bypass surgery is now established as the surgical treatment for angina. Reports from leading centres suggest that over half of those who undergo it, perhaps as many as seventy or eighty per cent, will be completely free from angina for months and even years afterwards. Of the remaining sufferers, less than half will be unimproved or worse. Some centres report that under ten per cent of patients fail to benefit from surgery.

The risks entailed in surgery have fallen steadily since the procedure was introduced. One exceptionally skilled team reported operative mortality rates for their second thousand patients of 3.2 per cent. It had dropped to one third of what it had been when they did their first couple of hundred operations.

Although the quality of life is usually improved by coronary bypass (so far as the cardiologists can tell), life expectancy is not. Indeed, the risk of death from a heart attack seems to be slightly increased for the first year after the operation, though the odds improve in subsequent years. For many people, this will be irrelevant. Even if their lives are not likely to be long, they would want their remaining years to be happy, rather than marred by pain.

Superficially, then, it seems that coronary bypass is a marvellous operation which should be gladly accepted by every angina sufferer to whom it is offered. But the situation may not be quite as it seems. There are many factors which tend to make the procedure appear better than it actually is.

First, we cannot discount the possibility of bias. The researcher, believing in the advantages of surgery, might tend to interpret his patients' reports of their progress in a rosier light than otherwise. Conscious bias is unlikely; unwitting bias is common. It is difficult to design studies which avoid the operation of this sort of distorting factor. Many studies have introduced bias by moving patients from one treatment group to another, according to their response to therapy. Objectivity is rare, medicine is always judge in its own court.

Second, the benefits may be attributable as much to a placebo effect as to the specific consequences of surgery. Placebo effects are basically the result of healing powers within the body. If anyone with a strong belief takes a tablet, has an injection, goes through surgery or psychoanalysis, this action on its own will frequently effect a cure. Thus sugar pills or injections of water can cure a host of ills; indeed, every therapeutic procedure is capable of producing a placebo effect.

The fact that the operation is currently fashionable – oh yes, surgery has its fashions, generally unrelated to patients' interests or needs – will add to its placebo rating. As will the commitment and faith of the patient. So will the demands of the procedure. The more painful the experience, the greater the good perceived by patients. Predictably, heart surgery produces a massive placebo effect.

We do not believe that the success of coronary bypass surgery is entirely due to the operation of such an effect. But it must be taken into account. It is enhanced by the strength of the patient's own commitment to recovery. It is as if the operation were a rite of passage into a new status group which permits a different way of behaving. Patients tend to work towards wellness in every way they can, changing their lifestyles to reduce the risk of cardiovascular disease. This has not escaped the notice of the surgeons. One review of the procedure published in the prestigious *Annals of Internal Medicine* commented that: 'Many patients, after experiencing the fears and risks of open heart surgery, subsequently change their lifestyles or curtail their efforts to reach high levels of professional or economic success.'

It is legitimate to state that many would not have needed surgery had they changed their lifestyle earlier. It is often true that a traumatic event gives a person pause, and that changes initiated at such times have lasting effects on the person's future. But these changes could be initiated at any time, and it might be that their long-term effectiveness would be greater if the heart had not been traumatised by surgery. Going through the operation may be a facilitation device; the risk and pain suffered giving a guilt-free excuse for subsequent actions.

If the person who has undergone cardiac surgery does not change any of the features of lifestyle that led to the development of the illness, the benefit is short-term. The new vessels will get clogged up just as the old ones did. Where scars mark the joins between graft and heart tissue, there is a purpose-built site for plaque formation. At these points blood clots and the narrowing which would tend to trap clots are more likely. The patient is back where he or she started. Coronary bypass is not the answer to heart disease, or even to angina. It may help for a while, what is essential is that the sufferer decides to live in such a way that heart disease becomes much less likely.

We believe that the benefits of coronary bypass surgery can be explained in terms of the changed lifestyle of the patients who have undergone the procedure. Initial relief from pain allows them to set about increasing their activity levels more rapidly than they otherwise could, but at a cost of increased susceptibility to heart attack while the operation scars heal. A period of complete bed-rest, such as the surgical patient gets, followed by a more gradual change in lifestyle, would, we predict, give better long-term results than surgery for all but a very small minority.

Other types of surgical intervention for heart disease involve the use of synthetic aids to heart function. The most important of these are pacemakers and artificial valves. Both of these are used to overcome the effects of damage to the heart. The heart valves are particularly susceptible to infection, especially from syphilis and rheumatic fever. When such infections were common, many people were incapacitated in varying degrees by leaky valves which failed to maintain the one-way circulation of blood through the heart.

Some unfortunates are born with incompetent valves, just as some are born with holes in their hearts and other malformations. For others, leaky valves are the long-term consequence of high blood pressure and congestion stretching the valves over many years until they are unable to recover. With ineffective valves the sufferer does not get the full benefit of the heart's action. The end result is lack of oxygen to the cells of the body, a shortfall which can become severe at times of high oxygen demand. People with leaky valves turn blue and feel breathless with exertion.

Today, plastic valves can be sewn into the heart. Between 4,000 and 5,000 such operations are carried out each year in Britain. They are far from perfect; the body tends to reject all such foreign substances and blood clots are liable to block them. Research continues to develop methods and materials which offer better long-term prospects.

Pacemakers are devices which provide a pulsed electrical stimulus to the heart. They can prolong the lives of people whose hearts have been so badly damaged by heart attack that the heart-beat is disrupted. Normally, the beat is initiated by a specialised part of the heart muscle (the sinu-atrial node), from which a wave of contraction spreads through the rest of the muscle. Heart muscle cells have the unique ability to contract in unison; put two cells together and they keep time. In the large mass of the heart the sinu-atrial node acts as the conductor.

If an area of heart muscle is badly scarred, the normal pathways through which this wave of contraction spreads are incapable of transmitting it. The pulsing of the fibres becomes disorganised, sections of the heart contract at inappropriate times because the communication systems have failed. The result is the same as the effect of heart attack; the muscle writhes ineffectively.

Electrical pacemaking overrides the individual propensities of the fibres to contract at their own pace. It ensures a steady, regular heart-beat. This relentless action is far from the natural action of the heart; the primary disadvantage is the inability to adapt to changes in need which would normally lead to changes in heart-rate. Pacemakers are marvels of modern science for which we would rather have no need particularly as it appears that a sizeable minority of candidates for them have had their hearts slowed by beta-blockers.

High-tech coronary care units were hailed as the answer to the sort of heart episode which killed Dave in chapter 1. Having spent many millions on such units, it was not long before disillusionment set in. In a study published in the *British Medical Journal* in 1971, it was noted that there was little difference in outcome if patients were taken to such units or taken home.

In *The Diseases of Civilisation*, Brian Inglis gave two insights into the use of these units. One was provided by Dr John Bradshaw, 'We rush him, bells a-clanging and lights a-flashing', to a coronary care unit where 'thanks to the stress of it all, he is quite likely to suffer a psychiatric disorder'. Psychiatrists, Bradshaw unkindly added, could then begin to study the patient if he survived the heart attack. In other words, heart attack patients were being subjected to 'variants of the very factors which we believe help to cause the disease'.

The second was provided by Professor Archibald Cochrane, who also discovered the 'doctor anomaly' referred to earlier. According to Professor Cochrane, when the result of the study which showed home treatment to be slightly better than intensive care was presented to a cardiologist, some joker had reversed the results. The study was roundly denounced as unethical. People were being condemned to die at home rather than being given treatment in intensive care! When the error was corrected, the same man could not be persuaded to declare coronary care units unethical.

The glamour of cardiac surgery focuses all its medical and technical prowess on the heart transplant. The operating theatre vies with the space vehicle launching-pad as the cathedral of our times. Both are directed towards infinite goals; the theatre to banishing mortality, the pad to escape from a finite world.

In Britain by August 1984, seventeen years after Christiaan Barnard's pioneer experiments with the hearts of black South

Africans in Cape Town, over two hundred people had received strangers' hearts. A few have had heart and lung transplants. The best publicised transplants, naturally, are the successes. Keith Castle, the longest surviving British success, celebrated the fifth anniversary of his operation for TV cameras in front of the hospital where he had his operation, drumming up support for transplantation. This has led some doctors, hard pushed for money for more realistic measures, to coin the phrase 'the transplant circus'.

Unfortunately, behind Keith are many who are not so lucky. About one in three of those who go through the operation die. Their new hearts fail; their bodies reject foreign organs; they succumb to infections and cancers as their suppressed immune systems fail. For most victims of heart disease, transplantation is not an option. It would not be appropriate anyway. Their problem is too generalised, too widespread through the vessels and organs of their bodies to be amenable to cure by replacement of the heart alone. To think of heart transplants as the ultimate answer is not only to misunderstand the nature of the problem, but also to misunderstand human nature.

Cardiologists are the best funded, the best publicised and the highest status group in the medical profession. Few question their judgement; even fewer seriously doubt their value to the advancement of the human condition. Yet, paradoxically, as more cardiologists reach the top echelons of their profession and more and more money and effort is poured into the battle with heart disease, more people suffer the effects of cardiovascular damage. As every year brings news of skirmishes won, the battle grows. The conquest of heart disease seems as far away as it ever was.

Heart transplants are said to 'capture the public imagination', presumably much as public torture and execution did until recently. This interest can only veer towards the morbid; it is concerned with defying mortality rather than a sound approach to health. With media acclaim and public fascination, the remit of the transplant surgeon widens remorselessly; from experimental novelty to weekly occurrence, transplants have moved on to heart and lung (perhaps in recognition of the market among smokers) to artificial hearts with three-ton backpacks. The latest step, the transplant of a baboon heart into a baby, had more than a hint of legitimised torture about it.

The skills involved are admirable, the technological refinements unquestionable and the devotion of the ancillaries that make such procedures possible magnificent. But is not the fact that medicine has to go to these lengths confirmation of a basic failure? If the front line provisions were correct, tens of thousands would not need surgery, and hundreds would not be driven to the final option.

The justification for even more resources being put into transplants is that all human life is special and should be saved. Nobody would dispute this; in a very small number of cases a transplant may be a reasonable option, perhaps the only possibility. But more lives could be saved for less money in less drastic ways.

When surgeons talk of heart transplants becoming 'routine', they are reflecting the requirements of their profession rather than the general welfare of their patients. Transplants are more an expression of social values than a realistic approach to personal health. Does drastic surgery on one part of a system make sense after the disease has run its destructive course?

A crack has appeared in professional ranks. Some specialists, provoked by the baboon incident, have commented publicly on the limits of their power. The ethics of the procedure were not their primary concern; rather they worry about the unrealistic expectations of parents with heart-damaged children. The acknowledgement that miracles may not always be possible may be the first step towards a more realistic debate on the whole question. Even the most dedicated enthusiast will ultimately be defeated by simple arithmetic; there will never be enough suitable spare organs to go around.

Of course, this has been realised. Dr David Bach of Harvard Medical School has suggested that the poor could help ends meet by selling their organs to the rich. A father could save his children from starvation by selling his heart. Dr Bach recognises that there might be an element of unfairness: 'We must ask, therefore, whether it is better to help only the rich or no one at all. The utilitarian answer is clear.' It is equally clear that the direction of medical effort cannot be left to doctors. How long before mercenaries, under cover of war, bring home bounty in the form of organs, or somebody starts to farm people as transplant stock?

We would not wish to deny anyone the chance of new life from salvaged parts. But pressure clearly creates moral and ethical dilemmas, where solutions lag far behind the advance of technical possibilities. We would be much happier with the whole question of transplants if only a small fraction of the money spent on their advancement was devoted to answering questions such as: Why are more babies born each year with deformed hearts? Why do more people suffer kidney failure? Why are livers increasingly at risk? And why do 300,000 people die of heart disease each year, despite all the measures discussed in this chapter?

And why do all ranks of medicine appear to prefer standing on the sidelines, waiting for illness to become established before they act? Why is their concern not to turn off the disease tap, rather than hopelessly trying to mop up afterwards? The momentum of medical effort has to be redirected if it is to make a major contribution to stopping the epidemic of heart disease. Until this happens, you have little option other than taking the responsibility of avoiding heart disease into your own hands. Put your life in their hands only as an unavoidable last resort.

CHAPTER 5

Life Dynamics

There are two tragedies in life. One is not to get your heart's desire. The other is to get it.

George Bernard Shaw *Man and Superman*

Our society confronts many people with Shaw's neatly encapsulated dilemma. As we seek those things that we imagine make up the good life, we generate a 'life dynamic' which too often produces a tragic ending whether or not we get those things we desire.

Life dynamics are the forces we generate by our interaction with the social and physical environment. They include the forces we generate within by our relationship with our self and those we generate by our relationships with others; the effects of our economic functions (the way we earn our living); and the sum total of all these activities on our environment.

As we act to generate these forces, so there is a reaction. Everything we do has some effect on us. Banging our heads against a wall does not only affect the wall. In questions of heart health, action and reaction can be subtle, but they are nevertheless predictable.

Hitting your head against a wall usually has an immediate effect, but adverse forces generated within your life dynamic can have a long delay built in. This is because humans are very adaptable; we can adjust to things which are not particularly good for us. During our lives we go from one not particularly good thing to another, pausing for a while to adjust before taking the next step. Steps and plateaus characterise many processes in our lives, including the descent to heart disease.

In this chapter we shall look at various areas of life in which the forces generated have a known effect upon the heart. We believe that these are the most crucial areas for long-term heart health. The next chapter contains questionnaires that allow you to assess the importance of these forces in your life.

Many societies, from the ancient Greeks to tribal societies surviving into our own times, have the shared belief that health depends upon harmonious social relationships, and that sickness inevitably follows social disruption. Our complex social lives are enacted within a world that is both shrinking and moving faster. Since we confront this reality with brains, metabolisms and bodies that evolved in circumstances that we would now consider almost totally alien, the potential for disruption is immense. The challenges and choices of modern life generate a state of stress in many people. Recognition of this has produced growing interest in various methods of 'coping with' or 'managing' stress. These tend to be superficial measures which fail to address the whole problem. Stress is a result of many factors, and it is not always a harmful one. To clarify the question, we shall define precisely what we mean by stress.

Stress: A state in which one or more of the systems of the body are working at or near the limit of their physical capacity.

Chronic Stress: People suffer from chronic stress when a state of stress becomes their normal way of living. The stress in this context is usually psychological.

Our interaction with the world about us produces stimulation, most of which we like. When we are stimulated and aroused to physical or mental activity, our brains order the breakdown of complex substances in the body which provide energy to fuel the activity. There is an either/or choice: either 'act' or 'recoup'. When we choose to fuel up activity, our systems suppress those recuperative mechanisms which store energy, use it for tissue repair and growth and deal with infections.

If we live in a way which leads to a predominance of a stimulated state, whether we regard the stimuli as 'good' or 'bad', the essential recuperative functions do not get their share of time or energy. We tend to become irritable, wearied through striving and prone to develop numerous minor infections.

When we are in the 'act' mode, the brain mobilises heart, blood vessels and kidney mechanisms to raise the blood pressure. This is quite normal. High blood pressure has come to be seen as a disease condition, but it is actually part of a complex of stress/stimulation coping mechanisms available to our bodies. When our blood pressure rises, we become sharper, more alert; we are cushioned against pain and shock; and if we are injured, it ensures that blood flows out to cleanse and seal the wound. Like all the other aspects of the 'act' mode, high blood pressure is intended to be a transitory phase. For the best long-term survival chance, our bodies would rather store, protect and recuperate.

But understimulation, too, becomes stressful. We get bored. We seek variety. At times we need to be highly stimulated, and at others totally passive. In short, we thrive with a balanced way of life, individual harmony dictating the extent of excesses in either direction.

A comparison of this ideal life dynamic with the way many people actually live illuminates the cause of much heart disease. Our very nature anticipates the varied conditions of the world in which we evolved. This anticipation is disrupted by the imbalance of our lives as we attempt to maintain a single extreme state for almost all of our waking hours. Heart disease has achieved such widespread proportions because our culture encourages distorted behaviour patterns, and we reinforce this encouragement – we find it very easy to become addicted to the fast-forward values of the 'act' mode of existence, despite – or perhaps even because of – their self-destructive content.

At this point we confront the two largest hurdles to heart health. First, many of the components of our behaviour which make us susceptible to heart disease are addictive. These range from nicotine and sugar to the adrenalin buzz that we feel when we take risks and the ego boost that comes of being the fastest rat in the race. Second, the amount of time we have invested in such practices gives them an inertia which can be difficult to overcome.

In practical terms, if you have been living in ways which promote disease for years or decades, it is unrealistic to expect to achieve any instant transformation; it will take time and determination. The psychological cost of such a reversal will be high; it requires acceptance of the idea that beliefs and attitudes on which your life has been founded are part of a harmful web that you have woven. It will take courage to acknowledge that you might have been wrong.

Psychologists refer to the sort of conflict involved as 'cognitive dissonance'. We constantly arrange our lives, our attitudes and our actions in such a way as to minimise dissonance, for it is a stressful state. But dissonance will arise if our actions fail to match our beliefs. Usually, people will adapt their beliefs to fit their behaviour, which means that long-lasting habits will be supported by a structure of attitudes that has an extra rigidity built into it by the need to avoid dissonance. This is why it may take a catastrophe like a heart attack or the experience of major surgery to produce a change in attitudes and behaviour.

We shall now discuss those specific areas of life dynamics which are known to be relevant to heart health.

Personality

Two American cardiologists, Drs Freidman and Rosenman, have carried out detailed studies of links between one type of personality and heart attacks. In *Type A Behaviour And Your*

Heart, they assert that fifty per cent of American men are type A, and therefore at risk of heart attack. The other fifty per cent are type B, and are likely to be all right.

Like most single definitive answers to heart disease, this is over-simple. Nevertheless, the tendency to behave in a particular way will have a predictable result on the individual. Roughly, type As behave in ways that involve excessive 'act' modes without adequate allowance for recuperation, while type Bs do not.

According to Friedman and Rosenman, 'In the absence of type A behaviour pattern, coronary heart disease almost never occurs before seventy years of age, regardless of the fatty foods eaten, the cigarettes smoked, or the lack of exercise. But when this behaviour pattern is present, coronary heart disease can easily erupt in one's thirties or forties. We are convinced that the spread of type A behaviour explains why death by heart disease, once confined mainly to the elderly, is increasingly common among younger people.'

This is not a totally new concept. In a book on heart disease published in 1897, the physician Sir William Osler wrote: 'A man who has early risen and late taken rest, who has eaten the bread of carefulness, striving for success in commercial, professional, or political life ... to him ... the avenger comes through his arteries.'

While not disagreeing with such views, we believe it is not rational to look at one facet of behaviour in isolation and use it as an absolute predictor of heart disease. Behaviour does make a significant contribution, but it needs to be maintained consistently over a long period of time.

Furthermore, it makes little sense to dismiss completely all the other variables that have been convincingly linked with heart disease. While it is possible to imagine that a slender waist (found by the Göteborg research team to be a very good predictor of heart health) reveals the existence of type B behaviour, we find it hard to believe that personality can be assessed with a tape measure. Nor can we dismiss the clear relationships between, for example, cigarette smoking, inactivity and life events and heart disease. We are dealing here with a complex interaction of forces, of which personality and behaviour form part.

No person is irrevocably fixed as either type A or type B. Our behaviour changes with circumstances, and with it the type of personality we project. The range of behaviour we are capable of is influenced by many factors: genetic predisposition, the way we respond to stimulation, our observation of the way others behave, and the sort of behaviour that has been associated with rewards in the past. Of these, the last two are the most important. They imply that it is difficult for somebody who lives in a type A society to become a type B. For all that, this style of behaviour is a matter of choice. When we change our priorities and the pressures to which we expose ourselves, our behaviour changes in response.

In the 1950s, sociologists studied leadership qualities in an effort to discover people who were 'born leaders', so that those with such qualities could be removed and encouraged. To their surprise, and against the genetic prejudice of British society, they found that everyone was a potential leader. Leadership was a matter of circumstances. In any group a leader will emerge; if that person is removed, another will take on the role, and so on until there are only two left, one of whom will tend to be dominant.

Type A behaviour is an extension of adaptive behaviour similar to leadership; under the right (wrong) circumstances we can all behave in this way, and run the risks that it entails. Conversely none of us needs to do so. So what are the characteristics which Friedman and Rosenman found to distinguish A and B types of behaviour?

A types are highly conscious of time pressure. They try to cram in as much as possible all the time. (Extreme A types will either have read this far at a sitting, gone straight to chapter 8 or junked the book because it did not give one simple answer that would allow them to continue as before but not risk a heart attack.) A types resent time 'lost' through sleep and rest. They are liable to push themselves to, and maintain themselves on the brink of, exhaustion and breakdown. A types seek stress. To them, not being in the thick of it is a sign of weakness. To keep in there they rely on adrenalin, to which they are addicted, to keep them fired up; and alcohol, to which they easily become addicted, to damp them down. Happiness is commuted for A types. They exchange it for the opportunity of doing more now, in the belief that they will be rewarded in the future – when they have achieved 'success'.

B types are characterised by an unhurried approach. They have all the time in the world, do not much mind being late or even missing things. (This lackadaisical style can infuriate A types, who see it as irresponsible. B types do not understand this, regarding As as unreasonable.) B types display habitual contentedness. They encourage a stoical acceptance which allows their tranquillity to remain intact. Paradoxically, B types may also become stress victims; whereas A types generate stress, B types suffer it. Under pressure they try to retreat; when cornered by circumstances they seek help, often in the form of drugs. Anxiety, imposed stress, a lack of control of their lives and the resulting personal unhappiness can be routes into disease for B types as much as for A types, but they are not likely to suffer heart attacks.

Few of us exhibit the extremes of A- or B-type behaviour. The important thing to realise is that directly harmful type A behaviour develops when inherent personality traits are aroused by specific environmental stimulation. It does not emerge without the challenge of our socio-cultural environment. What was originally an adaptive capacity has become inverted, leading to a stereotyped response and a loss of perspective. Dropping into the A-type pattern erodes an individual's capacity to develop novel and creative ways of dealing with problems. In our culture it has become the orthodox mode of conformist institutional behaviour.

A types find this hard to accept. They believe they are achievers with high competitive drive. This they take to imply intelligence, ability and a high capacity for problem-solving. These may be necessary pre-requisites, but they are not terms applicable to A-type life, which is typically locked into highly structured forms of minimal risk and high protection. The stress comes from refining corporate values at individual expense.

When beliefs and realities work in opposition to each other – as is usually the case when an ambitious person is clinging to the ladder of corporate success – the conflict produces frustration. This is revealed in type As' aggressiveness, urgency, impatience and free-floating but well-rationalised hostility.

The self-sacrificing, self-denying, self-destructive drive of A types that our culture prizes is rooted in a rejection of self. These people suffer from an underlying sense of insecurity that drives them constantly to prove their worth. Doubtful about their own value as people, they live by the values of business, corporations and institutions. Type A ideology is ultimately anti-life.

It is perhaps predictable that type As' most common reaction to the realisation that they are at risk is to leap frenetically into what they see as corrective action. They try to solve problems caused by excessive effort by making more effort. Because they have a fundamental misunderstanding of the nature of the problem, almost everything they do adds to it; they will swallow pills, perhaps have some surgery; they will exercise harder and faster than anyone else. To maintain what they see as their hard-won position they will attempt to solve this problem as they solve all others: by mastery, by defeat or by destruction. These strategies fail because the problem is in themselves.

Time Pressure

It is the front line troops in the battle against time who are most at risk from heart disease. This is not surprising. They are always working against it, they allow it to be used against them, and they abuse time by claiming they have none to take the action they know their health demands. The surprising thing is that this self-destructive army is composed entirely of volunteers.

The foolhardiness of these troops is notorious; they prefer to wait until disease and breakdown force them to take time. They may then adopt behaviour and habits which would have prevented the disaster, had the change been made earlier. Some die-hards are so locked into the battle that even a serious heart attack does not change their ways. They may make some attempt to get fit, but only to get back in there again. Eventually they are forced to take time – eternity.

When we are brought up to accept that time is money, it is predictable that we can feel guilty about wasting it. This is the advantage of the breakdown. It allows the victim to take time without feeling guilty. As we confront the post-scarcity economy of growing automation, it is yet another indication of the error of our social philosophy that it demands such a crippling price before we can treat ourselves rationally.

As individuals we actively contribute to the time battle-ground. We allow our lives to develop into a tight mesh of things we 'must' or 'ought' to do. Our duties to families, friends, job and social interests colour and capture every waking moment. Our assumptions of required standards and beliefs can reach the point where they allow no escape; we are trapped. Our traps can be constructed of peculiar things; while giving evidence to a divorce court, one woman told how she 'could not bear to think that the neighbours knew my husband slept in the nude. For forty-four years I have been buying pyjamas, then washing them out and hanging them on the line.'

Of course, it may be that we do not want the time to simply stand and stare. That unoccupied time can force us to confront things we would rather avoid. When everything is switched off, the tranquillity can reveal parts of our inner self that we would rather not see. And looking out to the world around at such times may prove such a horrifying experience that we cannot bear it for long. Many seek refuge in a self-imposed loading of safe trivia to fill time, implicitly trusting to others to pull them through any periods of crisis which may occur. The demands of 'duty' become an ideal refuge: 'I can't do that because I must...' People will exhaust themselves with furious activity which is irrelevant to the problem. But the problems do not go away, and there is a price for this refuge. It is a part of that price that we are seeking to question.

To promote health, command of time is essential. Some may find its unfamiliarity difficult to come to terms with. The unemployed, who have an excess of it, frequently find it slow and heavy. Some are weighed down by it, others find it elusive and slippery, never quite there when it's needed. Personal time needs to be taken slowly, little but often to begin with, and preferably for some positively defined use. Most free-time beginners start by doing nothing, or going for a walk, both ideal ways of becoming acclimatised. The essential ingredient is that such time is yours to use exclusively as you choose.

Exhaustion

Exhaustion is a natural state that we can all experience occasionally. It is a wider part of the cycle of human activities around the 'act' or 'recoup' switch in the brain. Once exhausted by exertion in response to events, we rest and recover until our systems are in neutral and ready once more. The normal cycle is daily; the depletion due to daytime activity is balanced by nightly sleep.

The exhaustion that is important in heart disease is chronic exhaustion, a state that builds up over a period of time. In chapter 1 David's heart attack followed an extended period of exhaustion. Because of imbalance in the natural cycle the recuperative systems are gradually, perhaps imperceptibly, left behind. Chronically exhausted people are those who have pushed themselves beyond the point where their systems can achieve a balanced shut down. Unfortunately, it is a state that is often not recognised by doctors.

The first step on this slippery slope is anxiety. Anxiety itself is a natural reaction, a low-level cautionary stimulus warning that something is not quite right. Anxiety should be dealt with by resolving its cause as soon as possible. If this is not done, it can too easily become incorporated into life as a permanent feature. Once embedded, anxiety can feed upon itself, we become anxious about being anxious, and the original cause becomes lost. Physiological changes set in and, even with no cause, we feel anxious all the time. Breaking this early part of the exhaustion state can be difficult. Millions of people are prescribed tranquillisers all the time for endemic anxiety. We discuss more satisfactory ways of dealing with the problem in chapter 8.

We have first to accept that anxiety should be a very short-term state. To avoid it building into something permanent we need to identify its causes and deal with it in some way which reduces the anxiety level. This may be by simply talking about it, or by writing it down on a 'worry list', on paper and out of mind. Anxiety can be recurrent, caused by long-term but non-crucial situations, a generalised worry about money or relationships, changes in environment, and so on. These should be dealt with on a daily basis; go over them before you sleep. Even the longest-term anxiety generators can be banished if you are gnawing away at them, rather than the other way round.

Difficulty in getting a good night's sleep is the next step. If you are fit and well, you can miss the occasional night in bed and soon recover. The sleeplessness that contributes to chronic exhaustion is the result of inability to wind down. An over-active brain can drag a weary body along in its wake; muscles primed with adrenalin can force a tired brain, through screwed up eyes and tension, into a headache as it tries to maintain concentration. Both are indications of imbalance in activity. The extreme occurs when you use will-power to force a weary brain to confront a situation with an exhausted body. In nature this would happen very rarely; in our society it is frequent, and an ingredient for disaster.

In many spheres of life we are expected to push ourselves just that little bit harder, to leave the 'act' switch on. Without realising it, we push ourselves nearer to a point of no return, where even if we want to, we cannot recover from our exertions, and the only route open is onwards to disaster. Dr Nixon has graphically described the exhaustion dimension of heart disease as being pushed over a catastrophe cliff. 'Axiomatically, a severely diseased heart is more easily pushed over its catastrophic cliff edge than a powerfully developed healthy organ, and a frail person is more vulnerable than a tough well-trained individual.'

He describes the situation at the cliff edge thus: 'The important influences that can carry the heart towards its catastrophic cliff edge are the products of rapidly switching and/or excessive sympathoadrenomedullary (SAM) and pituitary-adrenocortical (PAC) activity. SAM is associated with fruitless activity, rage and anger. PAC involves giving up, defeat and despair. SAM and PAC activity reaching self-destructive levels occurs most often in persons whose coping ability is gravely overburdened. Their struggles are excessive, their human support inadequate, and their morale undermined by lack of satisfaction and appreciation. They eventually break down.'

What Dr Nixon is describing is the result of that modern myth, 'One more push and I will make the breakthrough'. The dynamic of our culture conspires with that of our personal life to lead us step by step to the edge of our particular catastrophe cliff.

We can set up an unsatisfactory life dynamic which becomes self-perpetuating, self-reinforcing, and self-defeating. As Dr Nixon puts it, 'Life can easily become a battle to close the gap between what the individual actually can achieve and what he or she thinks is expected; the struggle is self-defeating, however, because the additional arousal pushes the individual inexorably downwards into illness.'

The process of extending effort into chronic exhaustion is illustrated by the human function curve (figure 4). Healthy exertion and recovery occur as we go up and down the front slope. As our capacity and ability are built up, the height of the slope is extended. Those at high risk are living on the back slope, somewhere between 'exhaustion' and the 'P' point, desperately trying to hang on. It is a hopeless position. Recognising this is the first step to getting your life dynamic cycling on the front slope.

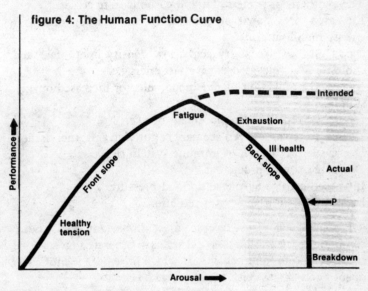

figure 4: The Human Function Curve

P represents the 'catastrophic cliff-edge' of instability where little further arousal is required to precipitate a breakdown

Source: Nixon, P. 'Stress and the cardiovascular system'. The Practitioner, 226, 1982, 1590.

Stress

Much attention has been devoted to the role of stress. This is probably because many of the symptoms it produces can be measured, a prime requirement for medical attention. Stress is popularly described as 'the stress of modern living', as if it were an unavoidable part of some ill-defined good life. The important thing to grasp about stress in relation to heart disease is that stress is a result of the way we live.

There are many routes to living in a state of stress. The most common is that discussed earlier, A-type behaviour. Time pressure and exhaustion also contribute. However it is produced, stress results in changes within the system of the body which have the following effects:

The synthesis of protein, fat and carbohydrate ceases.

Increased breakdown of protein, fat and carbohydrate for energy mobilisation.

Blood glucose, free fatty acids, low density lipoprotein and cholesterol are elevated to give fast energy.

Increased production of red blood cells for increased oxygen supply.

Decreased repair and replacement of liver.

Decreased repair and replacement of gut, skin and other tissues.

Decreased production of immune system cells.

Decreased sexual processes.

Increased cardiac output and blood pressure.

Increased sodium and water retention.

Psychological stress is the most important background condition for heart illness. It causes us to generate almost all the signs, symptoms and behaviours which have been identified as major heart disease risk factors.

High blood pressure and high blood cholesterol, the best predictors of serious heart disease, are both products of stress. They result from too much living in the 'act' mode. They are part of the physiological pattern of readiness for action, generated by our mental response to our lives. Prolonged anticipation of the necessity for action disrupts all the systems involved; like the sprinter held too long in the blocks by the starter.

If this response pattern continues over long periods of time, such indicators come to vary around the level appropriate to the 'act' mode, hovering in anticipation of a need for action. Return to neutral or 'recoup' mode levels becomes difficult. This is when fluctuating blood pressure shades into hypertension, with a consequent increase in the danger of spasm in blood vessels.

The way blood cholesterol levels are influenced by stress was beautifully illustrated by Freidman and Rosenman's study of accountants.

In the United States, everyone has to work out the tax they have to pay the government, and submit a tax account once a year. In the months leading up to this deadline, accountants work flat out calculating their clients' tax liability. With the increasing workload, accountants report increasing feelings of stress. At the same time, their blood cholesterol levels rise alarmingly. Then, when the deadline has passed and the pace of work slackens, their cholesterol falls. Struggle, tension and cholesterol rise and fall together.

Maintaining the stress-associated processes sets up a further series of self-perpetuating vicious circles, many with unhealthy side effects.

Stressed people seek salt in order to keep blood volume up to maintain high blood pressure in order to cope with stress. They may seek out red meat to aid red blood cell production. Red cells require iron, but higher iron is associated with arthritis, strokes and all the problems that accompany increased coagulability of the blood. Some stressed people will choose sugared foods in the unconscious hope of keeping blood sugar up. Cigarette smoking is usually a response to stress; stress is the most common reason for inability to give up and for relapsing.

All the processes described opposite are designed to supply instant energy and make the body ready for possible demands. They are part of the flight and fight reaction orchestrated by changes in hormone production directed by the brain, the emotional centres of which are directly connected with the hormone master gland, the pituitary. Adrenalin, cortisol, angiotensin and the other hormones concerned have multiple interlinked effects, each reinforcing the effects of others.

The majority of these changes will occur in anticipation of

external demands. You can be left simmering in stress in the immobilised comfort of your armchair. Energy mobilisation is quite inappropriate under these circumstances and, rather than enhancing your chances of survival, all these preparatory changes become dangerous.

For anyone caught in the web of high-stress living, untangling and untying the knots can be difficult. As we have seen, many habits adopted to help cope can end up by adding to the stress. Social drugs, such as coffee, nicotine, alcohol and salt, all end up as part of the problem, not the answer. Because of the insidious build up of stress patterns, our ability to acclimatise to them and the social assumptions which reinforce them, it is difficult to distinguish chicken from egg.

To take account of some of these complexities, we have divided stress into five principal areas of focus. These frequently overlap. This makes conventional stress management very difficult.

Metabolic Stress

Stress can result from a wide variety of adverse influences on our metabolism, ranging from allergic reactions to various substances to the effects of climatic variations and including metabolic inconsistency such as that produced by diabetes and pre-diabetic states.

Metabolic stress can be caused by the hormone imbalance resulting from constant 'act' mode behaviour. This will cause a disruption of digestive processes, hindering the fuelling and repair cycles of the body. Over time this is bound to contribute to degeneration of various metabolic systems. In turn, these may lead to increased susceptibility to heart disease. Mature onset diabetes is the most obvious example.

Once diabetes is established, the sufferer lurches from a state of excessively high blood sugar (hyperglycaemia) to low blood sugar (hypoglycaemia). The diabetic's life is a constant struggle to maintain a balance that allows more or less normal functioning. Stress on every part of the body due to these fluctuations is evident in the diabetic's susceptibility to many forms of illness, from infection to heart disease; and it overspills into emotional overreaction. Diabetics are notorious for their tempers.

Full-blown clinical diabetes is usually the culmination of many years' assault on the body by a diet high in refined sugar. Before it develops, the pre-diabetic person may become intolerant of sugar, with episodes of hypoglycaemia following sugar consumption because of an excessive insulin reaction. This drop in blood sugar stresses the body and produces emotional reactions ranging from weepiness to irrational anger.

Allergic reactions are also a source of metabolic stress. It is possible that allergies generally add a considerable weight of stress which is attributed to other causes, because the size of the allergy problem is not fully acknowledged. If people suffering from allergic stress are simply treated for the symptoms, their problem is likely to get worse because the cause has been overlooked.

Allergic reactions are caused by overloading our immune systems. In many ways our immune systems are like vast information banks on various molecules; their task is to identify every substance that enters the body and to set up a response that fits that substance. Because of the scale and complexity of the task, it is not surprising that the system occasionally malfunctions or becomes overloaded. This can cause auto-immune diseases such as ulcerative colitis and arthritis, vulnerability to infections, or allergies like eczema and hay fever.

The principle cause of immune overload is pollution. This includes not only the obvious and acknowledged pollution in our environment, but also the 35,000 artificial 'safe' chemicals which have been introduced into our lives over the past forty years or so. These are the ingredients of drugs, plastics, paints, food additives, pesticides and cleansers; no part of our lives is unaffected. These molecules are in the air we breathe, the water we drink and the food we eat. Each presents a possible problem to our immune systems.

Clinical ecologists have for years been pointing to the vast swell of sub-clinical malaise among human populations, which they attribute to adverse reactions to our chemical environment. The background of this pollution sets the stage for metabolic stress.

Increasing numbers of people in recent years have become concerned about the question of food additives. We have seen in chapter 2 how oxidised fatty acids in processed food may accelerate the degeneration of arterial plaques. Similarly, the preservatives, anti-oxidants, colourings, flavourings, hydro-lisers, enhancers, and so on and on, do have adverse effects on some people, as well as contributing to each individual's pollution load. They are bound to contribute to heart disease along the way.

Other sources of metabolic stress are the results of our attempts to override the in-built rhythms of our bodies. In the temperate zones of the world we have to cope with constantly changing daylight hours throughout the year and a cyclic climatic pattern. Even if we believe that the air-conditioned electrically-lit concrete habitat insulates us from these natural cycies, our bodies respond to their messages. In autumn, with shortening days and falling temperatures, we slow down and build up fat reserves for the winter ahead. Conversely, in spring, we speed up and become more active.

Dragging yourself out to work and coming home again in the dark does not feel right, and it is not. The inflexibility of a clock-dominated life overrides many of our natural inclinations and it has a price. Equally, the attempt to meet the demands of fashion by dieting to rid ourselves of our winter insulating layer will put a strain on our bodies.

We mentioned earlier the apparent anomaly of very fit aircrew falling victim to heart disease. In addition to the high mental demand and sedentary nature of their job, they have to cope with almost continual time zone changes. All our biochemical systems have innate rhythms; our hormone levels change according to the time of day and the season. Changing time zones means that all these rhythms are disrupted. We can think of nothing which is likely to cause more metabolic stress than living in a perpetual state of jet-lag.

Emotional Stress

We are all capable of a wide range of emotional responses to the experiences of everyday life. Emotional stress arises when our life seems to become locked into a pattern which produces predominantly bad experiences. Emotional disturbance is so common in the British population that it has been consistently estimated that around seventy per cent of all GP consultations are for problems whose basis is emotional rather than medical. We believe that emotional stress is probably one of the most significant and persistent threads in the tangled web of the heart disease problem.

Emotional stress provides the entry into many undesirable states which individuals might otherwise avoid. The problem is that it involves many intangibles; a life dynamic which gives one person all his heart's desires may be anathema to another. We enter the arena of almost infinite human variability in beliefs, expectations and response. There are many opposites which would stress each other if forced to live in close proximity: vegans and carnivores, the celibate and the promiscuous, Christians and atheists. The range of possible sources of conflict is as numerous as people. Dr Stewart Wolf, a cardiologist at the University of Texas, showed that clinically serious abnormal heart reactions occurred in individuals with apparently normal hearts when they discussed emotionally stressful topics.

Much emotional stress is self-generated. It comes from our beliefs or anticipation of the responses of others, and a view of ourselves in comparison to a picture of normality. Our beliefs about what is right or wrong, in everything from sex to the generation of electricity, form the system of values which underwrite our culture. Variations in the patterns of such beliefs produce the patterns which make cultures different from one another.

In the nominally Christian cultures of the West, guilt is the common foundation of much internalised emotional stress. We are conditioned to be guilty about our sexual nature and needs, and despite notions of a 'permissive' society, sex is still the source of much confusion and unhappiness.

Few of us are willing to conform with every norm of our society; to do so would mean living more like ants. Yet despite the fact that what unites us is more profound than what divides us, our divisions have the greater impact.

There are also forces outside ourselves which generate emotional stress. The phenomenon of future shock affects us all. In so many spheres of life things are changing so rapidly that it is impossible to keep up; we slip further behind becoming excluded, isolated and finally alienated.

Emotional health is both a product and a promoter of a satisfactory life dynamic. Achieving it can be a difficult matter; dealing with yourself and other individuals on this level is a part of life our society does not prepare us for; most of us are fumbling in the dark in one way or another. And it can be a painful process, requiring admissions which hurt, perhaps the acknowledgement that we may not have been creating the best of all possible worlds.

Change and Disruption

Any change, whether pleasant or not, is stressful to some degree. This is an area where we are particularly aware of the positive and negative faces of stress. We deliberately seek change in the form of novelty because it is exciting; indeed we spend large sums of money and many uncomfortable hours travelling in order to enjoy change in the form of holidays in unfamiliar surroundings. Nevertheless, holidays do put a strain on us, and few would want them to continue for more than a few weeks; not having one's familiar possessions, routines and environment means that everyday survival requires constant adaptation. The familiarity of the joke, 'I need to get back to work for a rest after my holiday', reflects awareness of the stress involved. Something exciting can be as tiring as something boring.

Pleasant changes, like holidays, new love affairs, promotion at work and moving to a new and desired home, will not precipitate a health catastrophe unless we are already overstretched. The happiness they bring is protective. Nevertheless, it has been observed that men are much more likely to have heart attacks in bed with their mistresses than with their wives; and travel insurance companies allow for a considerably increased risk of serious health breakdown when people are away from home.

The sort of change that brings sorrow is particularly dangerous, the more so if its effects are felt throughout one's life. Loss and bereavement can bring in their wake the strain of coping with a host of secondary changes. The man who loses his wife may have to learn about all the household routines whose effects he used to take for granted; he will have to see to all his own needs to a much greater degree than before. When he has lost all interest in such matters, this sort of adjustment may seem especially burdensome. Strain, a constant need for adjustment and grief take their toll together. Small wonder that many widowers fail to survive their first year alone.

The effects of life changes on health have been systematically studied by Thomas Holmes and Richard Rahe of the University of Washington. They observed that the stress of life changes was cumulative. The concept will be familiar to most people through unhappy experience: you might be coping quite well with one change, but if you then have to weather a second change, and some disaster hits soon afterwards, it all becomes too much. You feel you just cannot take any more. And that is when a susceptible person is liable to have a heart attack.

Holmes and Rahe have standardised a social readjustment scale which gives different weights to different common life changes, from which a total score for a specified period can be calculated by each individual. They found that people who scored highest almost invariably became ill during the course of the next year, while those with the lowest scores remained much healthier. The scale (p. 159) is a good predictor of illness of any type, but when many major changes occur within a short period, they are particularly associated with heart attack.

Stress-Inducing Behaviour

Driving is the commonest type of activity which induces potentially dangerous levels of stress. Every day millions of people sit behind steering wheels, highly aroused, with adrenalin levels up, remaining physically inactive. Even the sedate and theoretically regular progress of the bus driver produces high blood pressure, high cholesterol levels and twice the rate of heart attacks suffered by their conductors. This used to be explained in terms of the healthy exercise involved in collecting fares, but this was insufficient to influence cardio-vascular condition. When other variables were considered the stress of driving emerged as the crucial factor.

Dangerous activities will obviously produce stress – jumping out of aeroplanes, for instance. Even seasoned parachutists have heart-rates around 180 beats per minute just before their parachutes open. Thereafter, in relief, the rate rapidly drops. Of course, parachutists, particularly paratroopers, are expected to be fit enough to cope with these rigours.

But what about something like making an after-dinner speech or giving a talk to the local Budgerigar Club? Drs Carruthers and Taggart (the latter also a racing driver) carried out research on the sort of behaviour leading to heart attacks. As part of this they wired up public speakers to monitor their hearts while speaking. They found heart-rates up to 180 beats per minute, with averages of around 150, roughly equivalent to a parachute jump or sustained heavy physical labour. The same phenomena have been found with TV presenters and other performers. Few people who perform in public go in for the stringent training of the Paras – or even consider that it might be necessary; but heart attacks are common in this group. Coincidentally, Carruthers and Taggart found that the ECG traces of the speakers frequently showed characteristic abnormalities usually associated with a heart attack.

At this point we once more run across that earlier strand of our weave, type A behaviour. Under the spur of competition we produce A-type behaviour, using its short-term benefits to our advantage, but under sustained pressure we can become workaholic A-type personalities. For institutional urban man and woman the sprint designed for survival has been commuted to perpetual competition. Our closely structured world requires that we compete at each stage from cradle to pension, to improve our chances in the next; from home to primary school, up the education ladder, on into career structure, up the promotion ladder, to ... We get caught in a web that turns effort and competition into a means of self destruction.

Environmental Stress

As in the past, the environment in which we live is the most important background factor. Everywhere in the environment we have created, humans are in retreat. We are fouling our nest on a scale and with a sophistication unparalleled by any other species. The predictions based on computer modelling carried out for the Club of Rome and described in their important book, *The Limits to Growth*, indicate that humanity's story is just as likely to end in a whimper, choked by pollution, as with the bang of nuclear war. Some far-seeing people did not need a computer to predict this dismal ending for societies run according to Western industrial priorities. One was Chief Sealth of the Duwamish Tribe, who warned the President of the United States in 1855, 'Continue to contaminate your bed and you will one night suffocate in your own waste.'

Human activity produces pollution and environmental

degradation; human numbers make the options open to us extremely limited. The end result is a background stress level that constantly rises in our culture.

One particular form of environmental pollution is especially relevant to heart disease. It has been christened 'people poisoning' by Dr Peter Nixon. People poisoning is the stress induced by the daily confrontation of hundreds, perhaps thousands, of total strangers. In many ways the process is similar to the overload induced in our immune systems by having to confront strange molecules; as individuals we have, at some level, to assess and classify every other person we encounter.

Behind people poisoning lies the reality of over-population. Human numbers stress the environment to the point that many other species are driven to extinction; the same stress pushes us, individually and collectively, towards the same end.

Background stress is aggravated by our expectations. We are all propelled through life by a series of visions of things we expect to achieve, to have or receive. The more developed our society, the more we believe we are entitled to, and the more likely we are to suffer disruption of anticipation should these expectations not be met.

The wider the gap between our resources and our expectations, the higher the cost of achievement. The cost in stress and disease is well documented. More serious is the stress of failing to achieve major expectations. Much is made by some health statisticians of the adverse effects upon health of long-term unemployment. But the causal links are not obvious enough for the problem to be taken seriously at a political level. We must understand the possible effects of thwarted expectations, and develop contingency options and mental resilience as safe-guards.

It would be unrealistic to ignore the fact that at any time we all live minutes away from extinction. The thought of nuclear annihilation must colour the consciousness of us all. No matter whether your view is that nuclear weapons are essential for survival, or that they are the final products of a terminal culture, the mere fact that the possibility exists is enough for it to add to the stress of modern life.

All these contributors to stress operate by disrupting our anticipation of life. At many levels the imbalance we have created in our environment and in our personal and social mechanisms produces forces which unavoidably stress us. Human adaptability means that we try to accommodate them, but it is a strategy with limitations. We have to consider the possibility that our cultural evolution is now in direct conflict with our inalienable nature, and that to continue as we are is to invite even more casualties.

Control

We need to believe that we are in control of our lives. How far we are actually in control is one of those questions that is the philosophers' equivalent to painting the Forth Bridge. Their finely reasoned arguments need not bother us; what is important is our perception of our situation. Feeling in control is important because it implies choice, the conscious direction of our lives.

Very few of us see ourselves as one hundred per cent in control. We have to compromise, to trade off some things in order to achieve others. The needs to earn a living, to meet the needs and expectations of our families and to fulfil a range of personal and social responsibilities all require some surrender of control. Since most of our commitments are entered into voluntarily, they will not be seen as impositions. However, with the passage of time perception can change, as can circumstances and objectives. It is quite possible to wake up and wonder how we have built ourselves into the traps which suddenly surround us; life can become a cul-de-sac where imposed duty increasingly conflicts with desire.

Feeling that you are losing control of your life leads to stress.

This can be the result even for those who see themselves as in control when the effort of maintaining this perspective becomes excessive. The day-to-day demands of compromise and rationalisation can eat away at personality, undermining confidence, removing ambition and pushing options ever further into the future. We shut down, settle for the quiet life or simply accept defeat, while at the same time fervently denying that we might have got a lot of it wrong; this stress produces the familiar middle-life crisis for many. One answer is to resort to tranquillisers, keep up appearances, pretend happiness and for many to head for heart disease.

This uncertainty can lead to loneliness and isolation. For some, that most vital of all human commodities, hope, is extinguished. This is another route to the edge of catastrophe. If we are already overextended in attempting to maintain the fabric of our life, being badly let down, suffering the loss of a loved one or some economic disaster can be the last straw.

All these situations are governed by our perception of reality. While this may be a relative notion, very personal to each of us, it can be quite real. Modifying our perception by blanking our version of reality is not the best answer, although it can see us through the short-term crisis. Whether we use tranquillisers, alcohol or other substances, perception modification leaves the reality beyond intact.

The alternative is to change your perception; by so doing you change your subjective reality. This is, of course, how the traditional lunatic who believes he is Napoleon survives. We are not suggesting that you need go this far to avoid heart disease, but if control of your life is slipping away, you must start to think in different ways. This will help you see the harmful parts of your life in a more realistic way. Try thinking this way; living in a way which will lead to disease and premature death is nearer to madness than thinking you are Napoleon!

Altering your perception and regaining control take time. Such change is not easy; it requires first acknowledging the existence of the problem, then shedding some of the thickest protective layers we build around ourselves, those assumptions and prejudices which keep us on our old course.

Once parts of this protective armour are seen more as a hindrance than a help, the task will become easier. Changing back towards controlling your life will involve hesitant steps, and some will be in the wrong direction, but those which are right for you will bring a wave of energy and hope.

Activity

Physical activity is a crucial part of the heart health equation. Generally, increased physical activity decreases heart disease. This rule applies to all the various conditions involved. Today, leisure for many people means hours spent watching TV screens. This may relate directly to Professor Yudkin's discovery that heart deaths were highest in countries where there were more TV sets. A recent Sony advertisement underlines the point; it shows a worn-out sofa as testimony to the quality of their sets.

To increase your heart life the objective is to do enough physical activity to extend the front side of your human function curve as much as possible (figure 4). This will mean that you are better able to deal with things that you choose to take on, or that life chucks at you. You will not be forced into precarious survival on the back slope. As a bonus, you will understand better what your capacity is, because you will have actively created it.

We live in bodies designed for action. All the systems we have considered in our discussion so far suffer from underuse or inappropriate use. With all the many systems which interact within us to make us capable of the vast range of action and response which characterises human activity, one truth prevails: if you do not use it, you will surely lose it.

Our attitudes work against fulfilling this need. Perhaps as part of a misguided rejection of our animal nature, or because of aversion to anything reminiscent of brutishly hard work, or whatever, there is an effective conspiracy to deny our physical needs. This used to be true for those with 'weak hearts'; indefinite rest was prescribed, which led to further weakening. In society at large where motor-car ownership is looked upon as a universal right, the use of that right has become so widespread that the average journey is now less than two miles. With such values, nobody needs to prescribe inactivity. Even the growing interest in sport is likely to be most felt in the need to provide bigger car parks at the local venues.

If you wish to avoid heart disease, the case is simple. Sitting in a car or on a sofa with your systems awash with adrenalin is not good for you. Remember all those physiological processes that are hard at work against you while you are inactive. Effects of inactivity range from obesity and high blood pressure to bone disease. The prevalence of a wide range of such conditions in Britain attests to the poor physical shape of the population.

For most people physical activity means some form of exercise. Very few of us are fortunate enough to live a life which incorporates a sufficient range of activity to maintain a state of natural health. So we devise artificial substitutes intended to balance the artificiality of the other parts of our lives. There is no reason why this strategy should not work, as long as we realise that exercise is a substitute and guard against the inadequacies inherent in all substitutes.

The main danger of the majority of exercise routines or sports is that we quickly become acclimatised to the routine. When we started running, one mile was a target; soon we achieved it, then it became so easy that we could do it with little effort – and little effect. We were on a plateau and had to move on to something more to increase the capacity of our growing systems. Many of those 'once round the park' joggers are on a plateau, which for some is dangerously low. It is necessary to continue and develop our full potential.

The type of activity which is good for the cardiovascular system is aerobic activity. This does not mean burning with Jane

Fonda; ironically, exercise which produces this intense muscular pain is not aerobic. 'Aerobic' means activity that demands oxygen. It must be sufficiently sustained and strenuous to produce hard breathing, increase the heart-rate, and make you sweat. Activity that leaves you grey-faced, dizzy and sore is anaerobic, and it will do your heart no good at all.

Aerobic activity can be continued for quite long periods of time, and for peak heart health it should be. But many people find that a well-spent half hour, three times a week, is enough to produce marked benefits. Strenuous aerobic activity will put a demand on your heart. The aim is to encourage your heart to increase its capacity to cope. The coronary vessels themselves are capable of growing, and their central channels, the lumina, open up so that blood flows more freely through them. Such adaptations ensure that the heart continues to receive an adequate supply of blood under all conditions.

Once you are positively influencing the heart, the whole body will be sharing the benefits. Your systems will be using their capacity to good, rather than destructive, effect. And the benefits will be echoing through your systems for up to forty-eight hours after a bout of suitable activity.

One effect of sustained activity is loss of body fat. Indeed, only by increasing activity levels can we expect to lose fat; dieting, for all its popularity, tends to cause us to shed lean tissues – including that of the heart – rather than fat. With less fat, blood pressure and cholesterol tend to settle at lower levels.

Regular activity reduces stress levels, whether measured in terms of hormones, muscular tension or subjective anxiety. It improves sleep and combats depression. These benefits in turn feed back into the cholesterol control system and turn it down. Similarly, blood pressure rises with stress and decreases with regular activity. During activity, blood pressure rises with the heart-rate. Afterwards, in the recovery period, it falls again. In those with high blood pressure it usually drops to a lower level than before. The control mechanisms are complex, but the method is safe and cheap. (It is interesting to speculate how much the NHS could pay people to walk a mile or two, and still be in pocket through savings on the drug bill.)

The general good effects of physical activity can be felt in every aspect of our lives. Effort releases chemicals in the brain which produce the 'runner's high', an entirely natural reward for the good you are doing. Women who are active are less likely to suffer premenstrual blues and period pain; if they run enough miles they can even banish periods altogether. Activity also helps with painful conditions such as arthritis. And for men it reaches the parts other therapies cannot touch: surveys have consistently reported improvements in the sex lives of active men.

Once your level of activity is achieving these results, your body shape will be changing. This may be the first tangible sign that you are moving out of the risk zone. The change in shape happens in parallel with a change in content. You may weigh more or less, but the quality of flesh you carry will be improving. And this is a state you should maintain through physical activity for all of your life, whatever your age.

Despite all these benefits, media attention on exercise hazards has put many people off. When a well-known jogger or a squash player like Leonard Rossiter dies of a heart attack, the media cry 'We told you so!' and get an overweight doctor to say something quotable. However, there are hazards, and you should be aware of them, and more important should understand clearly what is happening to your body all the time.

The greatest dangers are for those who have an established heart condition. Consult your specialist and discuss the matter with him. Others at risk include: those who think they are fit, but are not; those whose intentions are good and enthusiasm is high, and who overdo it. And those who are very fat. If you are fat, make sure you understand the material concerning obesity to be found in chapter 2.

For everyone considering becoming active, the important things to bear in mind are these. The longer you have been inactive and the older you are, the longer it will take to get into a position where cardiac conditioning can occur. You need to get your body to the point where you can afford to put demands on your heart, and this means building up activity levels gently. There are no quick easy short-cuts. You must be realistic and start from where you are; the longest journey begins with the crucial first step. Lastly, do not suffer. If there is any hint of pain, rather than acceptable strain, stop. You must work with your body, to grow harmoniously, not batter it into submission. If you do, you will defeat yourself.

For all of us the ideal solution would be to restructure our lives so that a range of physical activity was included in our daily routines. Then exercise or sport could become a means of topping up or for pleasure. Many philosophers have suggested that we should be educated for a balanced combination of manual and intellectual work.

We believe that it is possible to achieve a way of life that promotes health by combining different types of activity. When we enjoy what we do, the boundaries between work and leisure become blurred. Such a lifestyle would include activities that demand physical effort such as small-scale farming, gardening, building and carpentry perhaps alternating with work of a more sedentary nature. With the geographical freedom that the growth of information technology permits, more and more people are finding that this sort of lifestyle is a practical possibility. Recent years have witnessed a steady exodus from the cities as people have moved back to smaller communities in search of a more satisfying and healthier life.

Try thinking of the question of activity in your life like this. If you and your family were threatened by a lethal scourge, you would obviously do everything in your power to survive. Heart disease is like a plague moving in slow motion. You do have time to act. It is a matter of assessing your priorities.

Happiness

Our final topic is the stumbling block of all conventional approaches to heart disease. While 'emotional well-being' is accepted as being important, it is usually limited to notions of a stable relationship, and fades out in detail much as old-fashioned novels used to...

Intangibles like happiness in the human equation are difficult to deal with; they are idiosyncratic and impossible to measure. There are no international happiness units, and without measurement it is difficult to increase amounts. What we can state emphatically is that the elusive state of happiness is absolutely essential for human well-being. This is especially true of the heart; it is no coincidence that happiness and the heart are closely intertwined in folklore.

Science, if not much help with the promotion of happiness, has firmly underwritten the notion of the broken heart. The evidence from numerous studies makes the link very clear. Here are some summaries of what has been found: Single people, whether single through choice, divorced or widowed, have higher death rates from all causes than the married or people in stable long-term relationships. For a young male, divorce is worse than being widowed. For those in the twenty-five to thirty-four age bracket being single produces a fifty per cent increase in the death-rate from heart disease, being widowed doubles the incidence, but being divorced makes it almost three times as common. Significantly perhaps, the overwhelming majority of divorces are set in motion by wives, not husbands. The highest risk for females is widowhood. In the twenty-five to thirty-four age bracket widowhood produces five times the incidence of heart deaths. (A nasty example of a vicious circle, if they were widowed by the same disease.) Being single makes these women three times as susceptible, whereas divorce doubles the risk in comparison with the married.

A study of identical male twins in Sweden showed no significant differences in smoking, obesity or cholesterol in the twin with heart disease. The distinguishing features were behaviour regarding work and leisure – especially problems at home – and a general lack of satisfaction with life.

From the other end, as it were, it is possible to use personal difficulties and depression as disease predictors. Using interviews and tests designed to measure depression and social frustration on 130 people (half of whom had heart disease) Texas cardiologist Dr Wolf – with no knowledge of which group any individual belonged to – predicted which 10 were most likely to die from a heart attack. In the subsequent four years 23 of the 130 people died, among them the predicted 10. All 'had failed to find meaningful satisfaction in social and leisure activities'.

Acute social isolation and loneliness within marriage are also associated with heart attacks. Dr J. H. Medalie screened 10,000 male Israelis who were symptom-free at the beginning of the study. During five years of observation he discovered that those who developed symptoms of heart disease tended to express more dissatisfaction with married life. Men who complained of a lack of social support from wives were far more likely to have heart attacks. This corresponds with other recent reports which point to marital problems and a sense of personal rejection as precursors of heart attacks.

All of these heart disease victims present a problem. If, walking down the street, you see a derelict alcoholic sleeping it off in the gutter, and a successful business executive stepping smartly by, which would you think is in need of help? One obviously is, but what of the other? Physical and mental degeneration can be seen, but the effects of unhappiness are usually invisible. Alcoholism, a social problem that is directly implicated in about 4,000 deaths a year, seems to cause more concern than heart attack, also a social problem – but one which kills twenty-five times as many. Perversely, the invisibility of the problem is made worse by the vehement denial of its existence by those most at risk.

Too often our society demands the projection of 'happiness', of an acceptable personality, a positive image. It is a built-in requirement of many occupations. The fixed smile of the chat-show host, the synchronised swimmer and the sales rep is acknowledged to be part of the job. But the cost of dissembling can be high. To have to pretend something you do not feel, to deny the reality of your true feelings, is to indulge in a particularly perverse form of self-destruction.

A healthy person will have a wide spectrum of feelings which will vary with circumstances, and should be freely expressed in interactions with others. This of course requires that the person be in control of his life, at least to the degree that he is free to be himself.

Inevitably, we all experience times of remorse, despair and even abject misery. If we live a balanced life, we are strong enough to cope with these transitory states, and all our emotions should be transitory, perhaps because they can be too intense to bear for long. Unrelieved misery is obviously bad for us, but unrelieved bliss could also prove detrimental. We require the contrast to establish our values, but in today's world it is easier to slip towards misery than bliss. Happiness is not a natural part of our culture; we have to work hard and consciously to build it in.

The Judeo-Christian backcloth of the Western industrialised nations requires that we legitimise our pleasure. Our capacity for feeling guilt has been institutionalised throughout history, and as a consequence most of us are subject to a wide range of inhibitions. Some are necessary so that we can live together and fit into society; equally many are not and only serve to repress us, their institutional base making them difficult to discard.

At their root such mechanisms derive from the need to safeguard experiences from the past which aided survival. In modern society they serve to protect the status quo by discouraging changes in patterns of behaviour. Despite this, cultures and societies do evolve and change. The problem is that unless we consciously direct this change, it is possible to become the victims of circumstances we choose to ignore. Heart disease in our culture is an obvious circumstance resulting from a lack of positive direction.

The directions of our society tend to be based on negative values. Britain is a notorious nest of 'old biddy-ism'. Much time and energy, under the guise of concern, is fruitlessly devoted to prurient observation and criticism of the behaviour of others. A High Court judge summed up the social attitude behind such activities nicely by remarking, 'Fun? There is no reference in any Act of Parliament to fun.' What a pity there is not. Spontaneity is rare, and looked upon as odd. We have got to the stage where the unexpected, no matter how pleasurable, fills us with anxiety.

In the recent past the evolution of our society has itself become imbalanced; the work ethic, the good of the state or company, the sacrifice to a higher cause, all take precedence over the needs of the individual. Heart disease and all those other intractable 'diseases of civilisation' may be seen as a result of this imbalance. Restoring the primacy of human needs and happiness is the first necessary step in redressing this imbalance. From this perspective we should be looking towards a world structured to human scale and human fulfilment.

The notion that our total life dynamic may be crucial to health is not new. It seems to be one of those ideas that was once woven into the fabric of our lives. It may have been lost, but many records exist of societies which used to understand the importance of the values we have been discussing.

The Iroquois Indians in seventeenth-century America were such a society. Their story below is taken from a paper by Peter Sterling and Joe Eyer on the *Biological Basis of Stress-Related Mortality* (published in *Social Science & Medicine, 15E*, 1981):

'The Iroquois Indians were a society of agriculturalists and warriors. The men were brave, self-reliant and uncomplaining even when subjected to physical torture. Although it was not permitted among them to express openly any weakness or dependence, the

Iroquois did dream. Their dreams were of rage – often directed against the French, and of pleasure – of feasting, of being cared for by friends, or orgiastic sex. Such dreams were entirely acceptable and as one account puts it, "without shame they received the fruits of their dreams and their souls were satisfied".

'It was understood by the Iroquois centuries before Freud that dreams are expressions of unconscious wishes. These were not, as the Victorians believed, statements of infantile conflict, but rather expressions of pressing adult needs. The dreams were publicly discussed and interpreted, and it was for the community to fulfil the demands of the dream. The Iroquois believed that failure to respond to the dream and frustration of its expressed wishes would result in serious illness and death.

'The community rallied round the dreamer with gifts and ritual. The dreamer was fed, he was danced over, he was rubbed with ashes, he was sung to, he was given valuable presents ... When someone had a hostile dream, he was helped by the community to act out the hostility – either in reality, if the hostility was directed outside the community – or symbolically if the object of anger was within the community. When a sick person dreamed about another person, it was understood that he wanted a friend. In such cases therapy included giving a friend in a special ceremony, following which the two treated each other as kin in a life-long relationship. In short, the Iroquois believed that disease could be prevented or cured by encouraging fierce warriors to be dependent, by helping members of the community to act out their fantasies, and by providing lonely people with friends.

'This view of disease as primarily a social phenomenon, the result of unfulfilled social or psychological need, is a very general one in primitive societies. It is also usual in such societies that an important part of therapy for existing disease involves restructuring social relationships to fulfil unmet needs.'

Have basic human needs changed radically since the seventeenth century?

CHAPTER 6

Assess Your Risk 2

The man that hath no music in himself
Nor is not mov'd with concord of sweet sounds
Is fit for treasons, stratagems, and spoils.
William Shakespeare *The Merchant of Venice*

This second assessment covers the topics discussed in the previous chapter. It cannot be as precise as the first questionnaire because, although each part of the life dynamic picture may have predictable results, when all the parts are put together, the interactive whole at best indicates only a general direction. For each individual the components will be different, but the total effect of similar directions will be roughly the same.

The questionnaire is divided into four main sections, with a final supplement. First, you should complete the appropriate section of the first three, depending upon your employment status. Everyone should complete section 4. Your score and its interpretation will indicate whether or not you need to complete the final supplementary section. Remember to keep a note of your total scores D, E and F. You will need them when you come to work out your personal strategy from chapter 8.

Most of the following questions take the form of a series of

statements. You should indicate how far you agree with each
statement by circling the appropriate letter:

a for 'very strongly agree',
b for 'agree',
c for 'doubtful',
d for 'disagree',
e for 'absolutely disagree'.

Section 1 is for those who are in work. If you would classify
yourself as unemployed (your personal definition, not that used
by any government body), complete section 2; retired and
others who are not in the jobs market complete section 3.

Section 1

1   How many hours do you work each week? (Count all
work you do because you feel you have to – eg earning income,
washing up; include time spent driving to work.) 42 50 hours

2   I really enjoy my work   a b c d e

3   I see my future in terms of career advancement
                                                         a b c d e

4   If I didn't have my job, my life would be empty
                                                         a b c d e

5   My job demands that I work faster than I would choose
to do   a b c d e

6   I have complete control over my work-load   a b c d e

Section 2
(To be completed by those who see themselves as unemployed)

7   Unemployment means constant money worries

a b c d e

8   I've got too much to do to take a job as well   a b c d e

9   Not having a job, I'm learning a lot   a b c d e

10   I resent the fact that I don't have a job   a b c d e

11   Unemployment is the worst experience of my life

a b c d e

Section 3
(To be completed by those who are either not available or not eligible for jobs)

12   I wish I could get a job   a b c d e

13   It upsets me that I can do nothing about the inadequacy of my income   a b c d e

14   I miss my work   a b c d e

15   My life is empty   a b c d e

16   I am able to use my time constructively   a b c d e

Section 4
(To be completed by all)

17   If somebody asks me about myself, I tend to talk about my work (includes looking after a family)   a b c d~~d~~ e

18   I fill up all my time with work   a b~~b~~ c d ~~e~~

19   I avoid work during the holidays and days off (check 'e' if you don't have holidays or days off)   ~~a~~ b c d e~~e~~

20   I don't have time to assess what I've done before moving on to the next job   a b c d ~~e~~

21   I prefer to do a few things perfectly than a lot less well   ~~a~~ b c d e

22   I have to keep my wits about me all the time   ~~a~~ b c d e

23   Work has never taken priority over relationships in my life   a b~~b~~ c d~~d~~ e

24   I have to do a lot of travelling   a b c d ~~e~~

25   My native language is the one I use now   ~~a~~ b c d e

26   I'm always having to hurry to meet deadlines   ~~a~~ b c d e~~e~~

27   I tend not to over-commit myself   a b c d ~~d~~ e

28   It's very important that I ensure the future security of my family   ~~a~~ b c d e

29   Money may not buy happiness– but you can't have much fun without it   ~~a~~ b c d e

30 I tend to assume I'll be able to look after myself tomorrow, just as I do today   (a) b c d e

31 I prefer a rather slow pace of life   a (b) c d e

32 I won't live in a city   a b (c) d e

33 Every day, I mingle in crowds of unfamiliar people   a b (c) d e

34 I feel I always have to pretend to be somebody I'm not   a b c d (e)

35 My life gives me neither satisfaction nor a feeling of accomplishment   a b c d (e)

36 I like to savour my meals and I won't hurry them   a b c (d) e

37 After meals, I resume activity immediately   a (b) c d e

38 I frequently go to bed within an hour of finishing my main meal of the evening   a b c d (e)

39 I haven't had time to worry about my diet   a b c d (e)

40 I tend to do two or three things at once   a (b) c d e

41 I recognise my limitations and don't try to push myself beyond them   a b c (d) e

42 I don't try to excel all the time   a b c (d) e

43 I am a competitive person   a (b) c d e

44   When I'm driving, I'll try to accelerate away from traffic lights faster than the person in the next lane   a b c d e

45   I would rather maintain good relationships with my colleagues than win personal victories   a b c d e

46   Even when I'm playing a game, I play to win   a b c d e

47   If somebody does me wrong, I'll do my best to get even
a b c d e

48   If I miss a chance, I'll brood about it afterwards
a b c d e

49   I expect a lot of myself   a b c d e

50   I usually find it quite easy to forgive and forget
a b c d e

51   I believe that our lives are ordered by a power greater than ourselves   a b c d e

52   I have to keep my irritation under control most days
a b c d e

53   I quite often cut or bruise myself accidentally   a b c d e

54   I despise people who are always wanting to take things easy – they don't take their share of responsibility   a b c d e

55   I don't give in to illness unless I'm really on my back
a b c d e

56   I give myself plenty of time to recuperate after exertion   a b c d e

57   I grind my teeth   a b c d e

58   I have a recurring tic   a b c d e

59   I feel calm and relaxed most of the time   a b c d e

60   I feel embarrassed if I have to ask for help   a b c d e

61   I laugh at myself readily – and I don't mind if others
laugh too   a b c d e

62   I don't tend to worry about what other people may say
about me   a b c d e

63   After all I've done, I deserve to be better off than I am
                                                        a b c d e

64   I prefer to get involved in long-term projects   a b c d e

65   To me, flexibility is more important than efficiency
                                                        a b c d e

66   I feel time spent on relaxation is time wasted   a b c d e

67   I find I snap at people when I don't really mean to
                                                        a b c d e

68   Sometimes I feel waves of anger sweeping over me
                                                        a b c d e

69   What I do is not appreciated   a b c d e

70   I feel I have all the time in the world to do what I
want   a b c d e

71 The 'mañana' attitude in some cultures would drive me mad   a b c d e

72 I'm frequently exposed to people who waste my precious time   a b c d e

73 I always allow plenty of time for things to go wrong – even if this means I miss some opportunities   a b c d e

74 A slow-moving queue makes my blood boil   a b c d e

75 I tend to be rather vague about time   a b c d e

76 When I'm listening to people, I quite often predict what they're going to say and finish their sentences for them
                                                a b c d e

77 I get impatient with people who do things slowly
                                                a b c d e

78 I spend a lot of time tending plants and/or animals
                                                a b c d e

79 I have at least one hobby or interest that I love, for which I will always make time   a b c d e

80 I like to create (compose/paint/dance/write/make music/improvise in any way)   a b c d e

81 It is important to me that I frequently touch and hold other living creatures   a b c d e

82 Receiving love makes me feel awkward   a b c d e

83 I feel I belong in the community in which I live
                                                a b c d e

84 I don't have any very close friends   a b c d e

85 The person/partner with whom I have a close loving relationship makes his/her love obvious even in public

         a b c d e

86 There are constant rows in my home   a b c d e

87 I feel isolated   a b c d e

88 I have a happy and satisfying sex life   a b c d e

89 I rarely feel like getting up in the mornings   a b c d e

90 Sometimes I feel I could sleep for a week, but I never get the chance   a b c d e

91 I suffer from nightmares   a b c d e

92 I have to override my tiredness and get on with what I have to do   a b c d e

93 I feel I'm running all the time, and getting nowhere

         a b c d e

Scoring

1   *Hours work per week*   *score*

Hours work per week	score
less than 10	0
10–19	1
20–28	2
29–35	3
36–41	4
42–46	5
47–50	6

Add 1 point for every subsequent 3 hours worked over 50 hours per week.

	a	b	c	d	e		
2	0	1	2	3	4	1	1
3	4	3	2	1	0	2	2
4	4	3	2	1	0	1	0
5	4	3	2	1	0	0	4
6	0	1	2	3	4	0	1
7	4	3	2	1	0		
8	0	1	2	3	4		
9	0	1	2	3	4		
10	4	3	2	1	0		
11	4	3	2	1	0		
12	4	3	2	1	0		
13	4	3	2	1	0		
14	4	3	2	1	0		
15	4	3	2	1	0		
16	0	1	2	3	4		
17	4	3	2	1	0	2	1
18	4	3	2	1	0	0	3
19	0	1	2	3	4	0	0
20	4	3	2	1	0	0	1
21	0	1	2	3	4	0	0
22	4	3	2	1	0	3	4
23	0	1	2	3	4	2	1
24	4	3	2	1	0	0	3
25	0	1	2	3	4	0	0
26	4	3	2	1	0	0	4
27	0	1	2	3	4	3	3
28	4	3	2	1	0	3	4
29	4	3	2	1	0	3	4
30	0	1	2	3	4	0	0
31	0	1	2	3	4	1	1
32	0	1	2	3	4	1	1
33	4	3	2	1	0	0	1
34	4	3	2	1	0	0	1
35	4	3	2	1	0	0	1
36	0	1	2	3	4	1	3

	a	b	c	d	e		
37	4	3	2	1	0	2	3
38	4	3	2	1	0	0	0
39	4	3	2	1	0	0	0
40	4	3	2	1	0	1	4
41	0	1	2	3	4	1	3
42	0	1	2	3	4	1	3
43	4	3	2	1	0	3	4
44	4	3	2	1	0	2	4
45	0	1	2	3	4	0	0
46	4	3	2	1	0	4	4
47	4	3	2	1	0	3	1
48	4	3	2	1	0	3	3
49	4	3	2	1	0	3	4
50	0	1	2	3	4	2	3
51	0	1	2	3	4	4	3
52	4	3	2	1	0	1	1
53	4	3	2	1	0	3	0
54	4	3	2	1	0	1	3
55	4	3	2	1	0	1	3
56	0	1	2	3	4	1	1
57	4	3	2	1	0	0	0
58	4	3	2	1	0	0	0
59	0	1	2	3	4	1	∟ 100
60	4	3	2	1	0	0	1
61	0	1	2	3	4	2	1
62	0	1	2	3	4	1	0
63	4	3	2	1	0	0	4
64	0	1	2	3	4	0	1
65	0	1	2	3	4	2	1
66	4	3	2	1	0	3	1
67	4	3	2	1	0	1	1
68	4	3	2	1	0	0	6
69	4	3	2	1	0	2	0
70	0	1	2	3	4	2	3
71	4	3	2	1	0	2	1

	a	b	c	d	e		
72	4	3	2	1	0	*0*	*0*
73	0	1	2	3	4	*2*	*4*
74	4	3	2	1	0	*3*	*3*
75	0	1	2	3	4	*3*	*1*
76	4	3	2	1	0	*0*	*0*
77	4	3	2	1	0	*3*	*3*
78	0	1	2	3	4	*3*	*3*
79	0	1	2	3	4	*3*	*4*
80	0	1	2	3	4	*0*	*1*
81	0	1	2	3	4	*1*	*0*
82	4	3	2	1	0	*3*	*1*
83	0	1	2	3	4	*2*	*1*
84	4	3	2	1	0	*0*	*0*
85	0	1	2	3	4	*4*	*3*
86	4	3	2	1	0	*3*	*1*
87	4	3	2	1	0	*1*	*0*
88	0	1	2	3	4	*1*	*0*
89	4	3	2	1	0	*1*	*0*
90	4	3	2	1	0	*0*	*0*
91	4	3	2	1	0	*0*	*0*
92	4	3	2	1	0	*0*	*1*
93	4	3	2	1	0	*0*	*0*

(114)

(140)

Score interpretation

Add together your score from section 1, 2 or 3, and section 4. This will give you Score E. It is advisable that you read the interpretation for the groups above and below the one you fall into. If you are very near the top or bottom end of a category, just read the interpretation for the group you nearly fell into and the one you are in.

If your E score was:

Under 70

Your immediate risk is very low, and your life dynamic not apparently far out of balance. You may be home-based, doing creative work or something that is your choice and under your control. You may be a house-person, or if you have a job it is one that you can cope with.

You can afford to take action to increase your potential, in health and life generally. Unless you are near the bottom end of the score, read the next assessment, and let it colour your interpretation a little. Use your current state as a foundation to build up long-term health; if you are young, resist habits and situations which will produce negative effects.

You should be alert to the possibility that your comfortable life dynamic could be disrupted by the fortune-tellers' favourite, unforeseen disaster. Develop a wide social network, and cultivate yourself; aim at fulfilment in as many areas of life as you are inclined to pursue. The wider your area of competence, the more resilient you will be.

Repeat your self-assessment every year or so.

70–130

Unless you had a high risk assessment in chapter 3, you are not likely to be at risk of heart attack. The pace and balance of your life are not far wrong, but you do need to be careful.

Your tendency is to put strains on yourself through an imbalance between duty and your emotional needs. This could put you into a potentially dangerous situation. When pressures mount, you need to keep cool, stand back and try to locate yourself on the human function curve. Do not let yourself be drawn into situations of higher risk.

The danger is of being caught in a situation where all your energy needs to be narrowly focused. Your best protection is to spread your energy over a wide field. This will probably mean getting involved in more social and physical activities, and keeping in touch with your creative side, but be careful not to overextend yourself into exhaustion.

The risk you run is that increasing pressure from work or duty could mean that you will cease to allow enough time for yourself and for recuperation. The important thing is to keep work in balance with health and pleasure.

130–200

Your life and attitudes are leading you into dangerous waters. If your score in the chapter 3 questionnaire was also high, you are definitely at risk; you must act now to improve your chances. It is likely that your life has been running out of balance and out of control for some time.

Part of your problem is your attitudes. You should consider the sort of break we propose for those in the next risk group: something to give you a different perspective on your life. Find a safe way to break up the protective shells you have accumulated. If you also find that you have a high D score (below), this is very important.

Your priorities need reassessment. Your ambition and expectations may lead you to put work before everything else. You should question this, be realistic about your real needs and likely rewards. Do you feel you have to prove yourself so frantically and at such a high potential cost?

You should aim at broadening your life and slowing its pace, restructuring it to meet more of your emotional and personal needs. This implies taking more time and energy for the things you want to do, and to develop a capacity for self-expression. You need to look inside yourself, away from the materialistic world. Look over those old inclinations and desires, travel, tilling the soil, building that boat, writing the novel. The essential you needs to assert itself.

While you do need to give yourself a better rounded life, you must not forget that you also need time to relax and do nothing. This might be essential anyway to allow you to rekindle those desires. Take at least half an hour a day that is yours, perhaps to meditate or get to know yourself again, in preparation for the change in course you should make.

Over 200

You are living in a heart attack zone. Do not panic. Even if you keep yourself fit and eat well, doing most things right, you are still heading in the wrong direction. Your life is probably speeding along, carrying the imbalances with it, but where is it going to?

You drive yourself hard, see yourself as deserving success, expect a lot from yourself, but find the rewards are inadequate for your self-sacrifice. When you think of this, the result is frustration and anger. Your lifestyle is too demanding, others seem to be having the fun and the fruits of your labour. You are left awash with unfulfilled expectations and dangerous hormones.

You need to step back and take a long hard look at where you are going, and why. Devote some of your talent and energy to yourself.

Your first objective should be to get off the back slope of the human function curve, so that you can start to build more capacity to live on the front slope.

It is likely that a sudden stop would not be acceptable to you. But consider going away into a different environment, away from all your usual preoccupations to give yourself space and peace to think over your situation. Keep doing this until you are sure about the direction of the rest of your life. Take those who share your life with you occasionally, and discuss the future with them, but remember you must put your needs first.

You need to rekindle dreams and desires, to take control of your life, and not be a victim of treadmills controlled and run by others. Quiet country inns with log fires, or gentle open scenery to walk through could help.

Your probable response to this advice is instant rejection. You may well think it totally unrealistic. You may argue that you do not have time for holidays, and anyway our suggestions bore you. If you care about your heart life, think again. Do you insist on being someone who will only take time for yourself after the heart attack strikes?

The problems in your life probably take many forms and will

not be easily resolved. They stem from your own attitudes and beliefs, and these are what you need to reassess in those quiet hours on the hills or by the riverside.

It may be that you have to deal with problems in your closest relationships. If so, look for help. Do not hesitate any longer. Effective help is available from such bodies as the Marriage Guidance Council, and you do not need to be married to take advantage of this help. They will guide you through difficulties of all sorts, including getting over divorce or widowhood and inability to form satisfying relationships.

Now could be the time for radical change in your life. Certainly you have to set some far-reaching changes in motion. *Warning*: take it gently. Give yourself ample time to consider – much more time than you would normally judge necessary. Be particularly sure that you are not overtired at this crucial time in your life. Remember that a sudden stop, an instant about turn, can be very dangerous. It might be the final straw.

The D Scale

As in the previous part of this questionnaire, you should rate your degree of agreement from a to e.

D1   I sleep easily and deeply through each night   *b*
D2   I feel trapped in my life – no options, little hope   *e*
D3   I find it difficult to maintain an image of myself as somebody worth knowing.   *e*
D4   I dream of fruitless struggle, of failure, loneliness, loss, illness or death   *e*
D5   As I've grown older, the world has lost its colour   *d*
D6   I feel depressed most of the time   *e*
D7   I really enjoy being alive   *a*

Scoring
Tick a if you strongly agree, b if you agree, c if you are doubtful,

d if you disagree, e if you strongly disagree. Those who do not have jobs should double their score.

D1	a=0	b=1	c=2	d=4	e=6	1
D2	a=6	b=4	c=2	d=1	e=0	0
D3	a=6	b=4	c=2	d=1	e=0	0
D4	a=6	b=5	c=3	d=2	e=0	0
D5	a=4	b=3	c=2	d=1	e=0	1
D6	a=6	b=4	c=2	d=1	e=0	0
D7	a=0	b=1	c=2	d=4	e=6	0

The D Score Interpretation   2

Under 5

Even if you are feeling the effects of stress in your life, you are weathering it well. Your very low D score will tend to protect you from any hazards that may have shown up in other parts of this self-assessment. Check out the risk category that comes before the one your E score placed you in.

6 to 19

Things are getting you down. Perhaps this is a transitory phase, the effect of some recent misfortune, or you are a person who has large mood-swings anyway and you are in the depressed part of your cycle. In any case, you should reassess your position in two weeks' time. In the meantime, make sure your life includes adequate rest and aerobic activity.

If you have been feeling a bit down for some time, you should look at your life dynamics. Most important in this context are social needs; perhaps you are lonely, or having problems in your primary relationship. You should take action now to remedy the situation. Depression should not be ignored, even when it is not severe or incapacitating. It carries a message which you must heed. Work out what it means, and act on this knowledge.

When you are depressed, it is difficult to build social relationships, but it is not nearly as impossible as it seems. Take-your courage in both hands and start joining groups. Advertise in local papers or special interest magazines if you are seeking other people like yourself, to whom you can relate. Or join an organisation for people with needs like yours. Some are listed in chapter 9.

Over 20

If you have been feeling this way for more than three weeks, you should ask your GP for help. He may not be able to do much himself, though some GPs will give you the time and opportunity you need to talk out your problem. Otherwise, ask to be referred to a psychotherapist, counsellor or similar professional. Do not allow yourself to be fobbed off with a prescription. Pills may make you feel better for a while, but they cannot touch the cause of your problem.

Some types of drug can cause depression. Examples include oral contraceptives and some forms of treatment for high blood pressure. Check out this possibility if you think it might apply to you. It may be that you have to change your medication or use a different form of contraception.

Read our advice on building social relationships in the section above. You might consider joining Depressives Anonymous if this is a recurring problem. If you can take a job – even a voluntary one – outside your home, which involves working with other people, do take it even if it is not what you would ideally wish to do. It is a strong protection against depression.

If your E Score was high (derived from the main questionnaire in this chapter) you are at serious risk of heart disease. Read the advice for the category below the one your score put you in. Depression makes you vulnerable to all types of illness, and heart disease is no exception.

What you can start to do immediately is nurture yourself. Think about the things you have enjoyed doing, the times you have felt happy. What features of these can you build into your life now? Do you need to escape more often? Maybe you should spend more time reading trashy fiction, going to massage parlours, having Turkish baths, or watching the girls go by. Let your fantasies roam everywhere and anywhere, just so long as you like the places your mind takes you.

Do not dwell on the awfulness of your life, or your unworthiness, or your despair at the things you have lost. Just start changing those aspects of your life that are tending to limit your happiness. Set yourself achievable goals, take small steps and work slowly but steadily towards a more satisfying life.

Finally, increase your activity. Physical activity really can lift depression and it can protect you from sliding into the depressed state. Walking, swimming, cycling, dancing, running – all of these and more can help. If you are unfit, work on this now. Check chapter 8 for specific advice. Physical achievement will build up a cycle of confidence and engender positive feelings about and within yourself. This will give you the strength to tackle more difficult areas of life.

We know that activity seems like anathema when you are depressed. We know that heavy, weary feeling. Our experience is that this feeling can float away with the stale air as you breathe deeply with the stimulus of aerobic activity. Something as simple as a walk round the park can start the process. Try it!

The Social Readjustment Rating Scale

This is the scale developed by Holmes and Rahe (p. 126) for the assessment of life changes. If any of the following changes have occurred in your life within the past year, add the appropriate scores together to derive your F score.

Event	Value
Death of spouse	100
Divorce	73
Marital separation	65
Jail term	63

Death of close family member	63
Personal injury or illness	53
Marriage	50
Fired from work	47
Marital reconciliation	45
Retirement	45
Change in family member's health	44
Pregnancy	40
Sex difficulties	39
Addition to family	39
Business readjustment	39
Change in financial status	38
Death of close friend	37
Change to a different line of work	36
Change in number of marital arguments	35
Large mortgage or loan taken	31
Foreclosure on mortgage or loan	30
Change in work responsibilities	29
Son or daughter leaving home	29
Trouble with in-laws	29
Outstanding personal achievement	28
Spouse begins or stops work	26
Starting or finishing school	26
Change in living conditions	25
Revision of personal habits	24
Trouble with boss	23
Change in work hours or conditions	20
Change in residence	20
Change in schools	20
Change in recreational habits	19
Change in church activities	19
Change in social activities	18
Small mortgage or loan	17
Change in sleeping habits	16
Change in number of family gatherings	15
Change in eating habits	15
Vacation	13
Christmas season	12
Minor violation of the law	11

If your F score was:

Over 300 points
You are at high risk. It is probable that you will suffer illness in the forthcoming year; you may already be aware of a health problem. Take things very easy, do not put any avoidable demands on yourself, do not expect anything of yourself. Look after yourself as much as you can; you are under considerable strain. What sort of illness you are vulnerable to depends on other aspects of your risk profile.

200–300 points
You too are at risk. How serious the risk is depends largely on the subjective importance of the changes that have taken place in your life. Obviously, the same life-event can mean different things for different people. For example, divorce for some may be a non-event; they may have been living effectively separate lives for some years, and the actual divorce is a formality. But others are shattered by divorce. Judge your vulnerability by the way you reacted to the changes of the past year, and treat yourself with suitable care.

100–200 points
You are not in the danger zone – unless the changes required considerable readjustment or were otherwise particularly stressful for you. Judge your risk of heart disease by balancing this score against the other scores derived from the question-naires in this book. If your other scores are high, you should take things easy now because you are likely to be vulnerable to the effects of stress.

Under 100 points
You carry no additional risk due to life change.

Global Life Dynamics
(a supplementary questionnaire)

If you sailed through the main section of the questionnaire unscathed, scoring less than 130, you should complete this final section to derive your G score.

If you strongly agree with any statement below tick a; if you have doubts or qualified agreement, tick b. If you strongly disagree, tick c.

It is my considered opinion that:

1   People bring poverty and disease upon themselves   a b (c)
2   The resources of the world are here for us to exploit

(a) b c

3   Everyone has the right to get as many of the good things of life as possible   (a) b c
4   The defences of our country should be stronger than those of our enemies   (a) b c
5   People cannot be thought of as animals   a b (c)
6   As an individual I am responsible only for myself and my family   a b (c)
7   Without controls, people behave irresponsibly   (a) b c
8   I am not interested in art or culture   a b (c)
9   Religion is essential for a moral society   a b (c)
10   Strength is a virtue (a) in individuals   (a) b c
(b) in people in positions of responsibility   (a) b c
(c) in government   (a) b c

Scoring
Calculate your G score from the following table:

	a	b	c	
1	7	1	3	3
2	7	1	3	7
3	7	3	1	7
4	7	3	1	7

5	7	3	0	0
6	7	1	3	3
7	7	3	0	7
8	7	3	1	1
9	7	3	0	0
10a	1	3	7	1
b	7	1	3	7
c	7	3	0	7

If you scored:

7–25

You are probably one of the people advised to give this book away after chapter 3. Your persistence indicates either extreme good health combined with concern, or you are a member of a caring profession. Your danger may be that you take too much of the troubles of the world upon yourself.

26–42 The supplementary questionnaire does not apply to you. You have been directed to it by the generalised nature of the earlier questions. Your repeat reassessment in the future should move you either up or down.

43–84

You probably will not have a heart attack; with luck you will also avoid serious heart disease. Nevertheless, you are living in a high risk zone. It is probable that you are a self-assured and very successful person. The problem is that your way of life may be actively creating the conditions which are giving so many people heart problems!

CHAPTER 7

Life Structure

He that will not apply new remedies
must expect new evils;
for time is the greatest innovator.

Francis Bacon Of Innovators

Life structure is that dimension of our being within which our life dynamics and lifestyle are contained. It consists of those broad influences outside our ship: the equivalents of the deep ocean currents, the climatic cycles and those wider immutable factors which are a part of our planetary environment. Ignoring the fact that we are essentially land-based creatures is something we do at a price.

Discussion of such influences will inevitably seem to move us away from the details of what might be specifically good for the heart. The influences which help to produce unhealthy cardiovascular systems also promote the spread of other intractable diseases throughout our society.

The relevance of our life structure needs to be considered from two positions. One is the structure of our planetary environment, and our place within its web of life. The other is the fine detail of ways in which we may be constrained to live as a part of that web. Humans are noted for their ability to overcome constraints. We are continually expanding the frontiers of our knowledge and experience, and any appeal to pull back, to stop, is likely to be pointless, whatever the cost in death or suffering. We will go onward, it is a part of our nature.

Given this, we are not in any way going to advise that you attempt consciously to restrict your part of the human adventure. If this were a necessary prerequisite for improving your chances of a longer life, it would largely be ignored. What we will say is that it is important for you, as for any other life form, to recognise the nature of the boundaries of your existence.

It is desirable to be aware of the effects of such boundaries, and to be realistic about your abilities in relation to demands they may impose. As a very crude illustration of the sort of perspective we are aiming for, nobody would expect a cheetah to be a good long-distance swimmer, or a dolphin to run a marathon. Their life structures will not allow them to transcend their environmental limitations.

We have learned to use technology to overcome many of our natural limitations, and because we are so good at adapting and extending our personal capacities the possibility of overreaching important limits has been obscured. It is not that new technology is necessarily bad, but that it encourages us, perhaps too easily, to discard all of the old without a true appreciation of its worth.

Indiscriminate acceptance of the fruits of innovation is matched by the movement of heart disease through the age-scale and into populations that used to be free of it. We like novelty, but we are slow to appreciate the hidden costs and subtle consequences. The twentieth-century love affair with the motor car is a good example.

Obviously, cars do not directly cause heart disease. (We could debate the effects of exhaust emissions, but at the moment that is a secondary consideration.) For many people the way they live would be impossible without a car, and for long-distance travel with kids and pets and their accompanying paraphernalia they are so far unbeatable. Man has developed an exoskeletal shell inside which he can pack all his genetic preoccupations. The car has also given the most ordinarily unfit the speed, comfort and illusions of grandeur that fantasies are made of. Even in the crowded poverty of the third world shanty town a car is the symbol of affluence and power.

Car ownership has led some people to regard walking as inferior to driving. They imagine that their children are somehow deprived if not driven to and from a school that is within easy walking distance. We regard cars as convenient while disregarding the damage that we can do to ourselves, our children and the environment by our excessive use of them.

For many people, it looks as if heart disease is inevitable. At the deepest level, could this be the unpalatable truth of the matter? Are we forced to accept that, while measures to improve heart life will be beneficial to a certain percentage of people, there will remain a growing residue who will experience no benefit. Could there be some deeply susceptible people who provide an indication of what an unmodified future will hold for growing numbers? Or could such an analysis of the pressures that affect these people be used to create a general health improvement among entire populations?

Of necessity, this approach will produce a very broad-brush picture. Benefit from this exploration cannot be considered in terms of a simple prescription such as 'eat less fat'. Rather we are now dealing with a wide general awareness; the growth of a personal understanding of the nature of our relationship with ourselves, our dependence on recognition of boundaries of possibility, the effects of overcoming them – in short, our interaction with ourselves, our species and all life on this planet.

To begin this exploration we have to take a large step back and look at our species with dispassionate eyes, much as an alien scientist might. After being suitably impressed by the display of health and strength at the Los Angeles Olympics, our alien might suffer some disillusionment when looking at the global state of humanity. All the contradictions of the human condition, including those traced in our journey through the causes of heart disease, would become apparent.

Where would our alien begin? The best bet would be to go

back in time, then scan forward to trace the development of the situation. This should show up key events which would allow some interpretation of causes, and indicate the options available for corrective action.

Two million years ago, small groups of people, essentially the same as us, would be found living in small tribal groups. They populated lake and riverside habitats in the sub-tropical zones. The plants and animals which shared their environment were species which are familiar to us. It is reasonable to suppose that their preoccupations were very similar to ours: children, food, personal relationships, security, happiness and so on. It was in the way in which they fulfilled their needs that they differed from us, not fundamentally, but certainly in ways that are significant.

They lived by gathering and hunting. The women were at the core of this society, working in cohesive groups gathering food from a range of static sources: nuts, fruits and roots, eggs and insects. This activity blended well with the demands of child care. Elders would be at hand to pass on the benefits of skill and experience. Being more expendable to the species, men would roam on the perimeter of the group, to provide warning or protection, to scavenge and hunt.

The dependable provision gathered by the women formed an adequate protein base, and the occasional inclusion of meat from the activity of the men supplemented this with a high energy food. Our diet had other advantages which may go some way to explain the most significant evolutionary change that was under way at this time: our brains were increasing steadily in size.

This picture of the life of our distant ancestors is a composite, derived from observation of the few remnants of humanity who still live as gatherer hunters today, and painstaking interpretation of prehistoric remains. One factor to emerge, both from studies and re-creation, is that in suitable environments people can provide for all their essential needs with between two and four hours' work each day. Their lives were characterised by sharing, co-operation and leisure. Our gatherer/hunter past has been described as the first affluent society, not because of material possessions, but because of its leisure time.

What would our alien see as important in the way these people lived? Probably that the core group of females would form the decision power base; it is likely that they decided who should breed with whom and when, and their knowledge of cyclic phenomena, such as the seasons of plants, would govern the group's roaming pattern. The strong verbal tradition among the women would develop and pass on the historical record and wisdom of the tribe. The male role would be seen to be slightly more complicated.

To improve their chances of breeding men had to distinguish themselves in the eyes of the females, either by bravery, foolhardiness, by being a good, aggressive hunter, or by displaying some exceptional characteristic. Almost all of these activities are characterised by risk. And here we have the essence of the evolutionary trap for the male; to breed he has to take risks, yet he also has to survive. Men have to be distinct from their fellows, yet they depend upon each other for co-operative ventures. Being able to cope with these contradictory demands marked those suited to pass on their genes. Somewhere in the capacity to cope with such contradictions is the root of modern man's ability to accept a high-stress way of life. It is an ability which has become fatally overdeveloped in the situation modern economic man confronts today.

For around one and a half million years little changed. Human numbers remained remarkably stable, although, as a species, we were not a part of another's food chain and had no specific predators. Throughout this long stable epoch of our prehistory it has been estimated that human numbers remained between one and five millions.

Roughly half a million years ago a subtle change was underway. Humans began to disperse to less favourable areas of the planet, with harsher climates and more seasonal variation in food supplies. The reasons for this are open to speculation.

Nothing profound seems to have occurred to inspire it, and it was not accompanied by any major evolutionary development.

Around twenty thousand years ago humanity settled to agriculture. Settlement was probably the most profound change in human history. It marked the beginning of our disassociation with the natural environment. Until the age of settlement we had been symbiotically integrated with all the planetary systems; settlement marked the beginning of domination and change. The imposition of human will upon the environment was to have repercussions upon us as well as on our world. As Jonas Salk, the inventor of the polio vaccine, observed, 'We are participants in the evolutionary process: we are victims of the effects we cause.'

One effect of settlement was the reversal of the social roles between men and women. The gatherer groups were disbanded. From providing the cohesive base for the tribal group, women became *de facto* breeding stock, as important to the hunter turned farmer as his other livestock. The dislocation of life away from the supportive group is a change which women are still suffering from today. The resultant stress can take forms for which tranquillisers or beta-blockers are prescribed.

Agriculture gave men a purpose. It also provided a more certain means of reproduction, and made it important to know which were their sons. Inheritance of the investment of time, the possession of land and the ownership of stock had replaced a carefree existence characterised by a perhaps unfulfilling leisure. The hunter had become the farmer, the lawyer, the politician, the priest and the soldier.

Lest the events of twenty thousand years ago seem totally irrelevant to making the most of options for living today, it is important to get some perspective of the time scale involved. What is most relevant is not the spectacular and perhaps alarming increasing rate of change that we experience now, but the fact that ninety-nine per cent of the time our species has existed was spent in the low density stable structural pattern of gatherer hunter tribal societies. If we take two million years, roughly the time *Homo sapiens* has existed on this planet, then we have lived as settled agriculturalists for only 1% of our species time span. We have been fossil-fuel technologists for .01% and electronic computer technologists for .001% of our time. Yet, despite the rapidity of the changes in our recent past, we remain essentially the same physical beings that our alien first found. Our evolutionary trail from the Miocene, the age of the apes some seventeen million years ago, was substantially completed around three million years ago.

What are the implications of our stable post-evolutionary past, and what is the relevance of the changes of the latest 1% of our time span? We need to recognise the endurance of the way our bodies and minds have evolved and lived within the ecology of the planet. Whatever the changes we have wrought, and wherever our intelligence and imagination may carry us, we are still connected to the reality of that evolution. And we are as dependent upon it as the tallest tree is dependent on its roots remaining in suitable soil.

Dismissing the needs of our human heritage, either wilfully or through a lack of understanding, has costs. Every degree of disassociation leads us nearer to some potential for disrupting our built-in anticipation of those needs. We do not need to live like cave dwellers to fulfil all our anticipated needs, but we do need to be very clear about which we can ignore and which are essential to our well-being. Progress has costs which we tend to overlook in our enthusiasm for its apparent benefits. If we are not sufficiently circumspect in our assessment, the costs can rapidly accumulate. One deficit we all currently bear is the epidemic of 'diseases of civilisation'.

Obviously we cannot go back. A return to an earlier state is an evolutionary impossibility, whether or not it may be considered desirable. The ultimate choice, one which we all wish to avoid, is between our continuation or annihilation. But unless we are prepared to keep the welfare of humanity permanently on the agenda, that choice remains our only option, with the gap between the two shrinking as our passivity weighs the odds increasingly in favour of the latter.

This conflict confronts us with the macro-elements at work in our life structure. If as individuals we have changed little in measurable ways during our recent past, this does not mean that evolution has stopped. In fact, rather the reverse; it has speeded up. We are subjecting ourselves to a rapid and apparently accelerating rate of change. To be able to make meaningful choices we need to explore the source of this accelerated change, and clarify its implications for us as individuals.

Evolution is conventionally thought of in terms of biological development. This is inappropriate for humans; we have progressed far beyond our biological limitations. So much so that the characteristic which differentiates us from any other life-form may be that we are the first species to evolve beyond our purely genetic potential.

Today we are dependent upon social and cultural mechanisms which have evolved in our recent past. Few of us could survive if the artifacts of our society were to disappear overnight. But our dependence is deeper than the obvious material and energy inputs we require. Humans need to be a part of a culture; to share values, beliefs and experiences, to have a common understanding of life with their fellows. Those brains which continually increased in size as the latest manifestation of our physical evolution demand the involvement and use that cultured living provides.

Our interaction with our culture is a mutual experience. We are nurtured within its values and opportunities, and as we grow, we in our turn contribute to the growth of our culture. Each generation adds to its growth and accumulation. The degree to which we comply with the values and demands of our various cultures would lead our alien seriously to question the validity of our concept of 'individuality'.

The net result of our social evolution and its culture is that, within our cultural cocoon, we live our lives on the basis of assumptions. Against the backcloth of culture, our assumptions are based on a variety of influences. These range from the traditional ways things have been done, what we regard as 'normal', the choices made by our peers and the things we may be persuaded to accept. We pick up fragments of knowledge, opinion and observation and blend them with our inclinations to produce modes of behaviour and ways of thinking. Our beliefs are generally regarded as objective truth.

This assumptive behaviour maintains our social fabric. It is not necessarily based on fact, or rational analysis, or obvious benefit; it simply allows large numbers of people to live together fairly agreeably because of their shared view of reality. To return to our ship model of the disease processes, we may have to accept that our cultural ship has more in common with the *Titanic* than those of us dancing in the elegant salons of Western life would care to realise.

The entirely arbitrary nature of our social norms can be seen by considering other societies. Foreigners are frequently to be found doing things which we find almost unthinkable, yet they seem quite happy and oddly find no reason to question their own behaviour. The values which cause such behaviour are far from arbitrary for the individuals involved. It is almost impossible to break with the culture that nurtures us. This explains why there are few communists in America, the Jewish faith is not popular in Ireland or Catholicism in Israel, and capitalism is difficult in Russia.

Making choices about our life structure becomes difficult if it involves going against our social assumptions. The degree of difficulty relates to the importance of the choice, to the effect it will have on society at large. Within a sophisticated culture there will be areas where the divergences of our anticipated needs and the momentum of the culture will be marked.

The problem can be illustrated by considering margarine. You may decide, having considered all the evidence, to give up eating butter in favour of an unsaturated vegetable fat margarine. If you live on your own, there will be no problem. If on the other hand, your family prefers butter, you will be aware of currents of pressure or inconvenience arising as a result of your choice. If many people make the same choice, and butter sales start to fall, you will come under pressure from the dairy industry. This will range from the 'tut-tut' of the shopkeeper, to the media warfare of the advertising industry, seeking to persuade a percentage of people to change their minds.

If the switch to margarine became universal, it would cause major problems. Butter prices would be lowered, it would be given free to pensioners, and if the Russians could not be persuaded to take more and the Euro butter mountain backed up to the point where the farming community was disrupted, serious political action would have to be taken. It would then become your patriotic duty to eat butter, and to encourage your family and friends to do likewise.

An individual choice, based on reason, would only encounter mild opposition. When tens of thousands make the same choice, it becomes an industrial and economic battle for your heart and mind. If millions make the choice, it becomes a question of politics. The important thing to notice about this escalation is that beyond the first level – the choice of the individual – questions of reason and health will not arise. Factors to do with social values rapidly take over and attempt to negate any notion of individual good.

To question the validity of individual choice is crucial to our efforts to avoid heart disease. To what degree are we free individuals with effective choice over our life structure, or to what degree are we embedded in our culture and victims of its adverse effects? Can we expect to structure our lives within our culture in a way that will improve our heart life and health, or must we accept that there are tides and currents in the nature of humanity to which we are helpless victims?

The answer to these questions lies in the very nature of the structures human society produces. These fall into two categories: those of which we are conscious, and those of which we are a part, but of which we are unaware. Both are derived from inherent qualities in our nature.

Human co-operation has produced a variety of organisations in the modern world, ranging from local clubs to multinational business corporations, nation states and their international organisations. All had their origins in the fulfilment of a purpose to serve a perceived human need. There are some cultural differences in the sort of organisation and its administrative details evolved to fulfil these needs, but by and large the results are very similar.

The source of these organisational structures is in the morphology of our species. Literally, morphology means 'shape', and this is a reasonable notion from which we can develop the idea. If you were to take a couple of mice and let them loose in your house, the results would be fairly predictable. They would find an inaccessible nook to build their nest, lay out scent runs to food sources and other necessities, have a battle of wits with you over your food and breed rapidly. Their behaviour would be typical of their species, they would produce all the manifestations of existence that we associate with mice. Their total presence within the environment is their morphology, the shape of their existence.

If you have a cat, there will be a clash with the mice. The antagonism of their morphologies will probably ensure that the mice keep a very low profile. If the mice breed fast enough to feed the cat, they will exist in balance. If your cat has kittens, the demand on the mice may lead to their extermination. This brief overextension of the cat morphology may also lead to its demise in the absence of suitable food. For both balance is the answer.

We must obviously be cautious about extending lessons from the observation of animals directly to human situations. Equally, we would be worse than foolish to discount the implications. The global human population has increased by fifty per cent in the last twenty-five years; it will probably double before the end of this century. Under these circumstances, it is little wonder that we yearn to restore many elements of our very recent past, and also understandable that what was important in those long stable eons of balanced living tends to become lost in our headlong explosion.

Our numbers are compressing and distorting human morphology as surely as overcrowding distorts that of animals. The fact that we are more complex and adaptable only obscures the effects, but finally they emerge. People poisoning is accepted as a stress factor in heart disease, and our adaptability has not solved the problem of isolation and despair amid the numbers in large cities.

Human ingenuity has been directed towards solving environmental problems which hindered our advance. We are the mice who sorted out the cats in a way which tells us something about ourselves. It also brings us to the final problem of our life structure.

In our gatherer hunter past we exhibited a highly developed capacity for co-operation. Since this way of living was unencumbered, the co-operation was directed to fulfilling immediate needs. With settlement came the notions of possession and investment; in addition to the reversal of sexual dynamics, our social evolution went through a further inversion – 'ours' became 'mine'.

Men began to devise methods of protecting their land and property. At its crudest this was by simple violence, but in time it was by the sophistication of the social accords that were developed. Most of the assumptions to which we now subscribe have their origins in this inversion; private property, ownership, the notion that a person, or his genetic descendants, can have exclusive use of a part of the planet. This left us with the nuclear family, the disassociation of the bond structure of group and tribe, and the notion of individual responsibility.

The values that emerged from these social changes required long-term stability. A man had to be sure that what he had gained during his lifetime would be passed on to his heirs. The mechanisms of society became institutionalised. The values of society were thus established in a way that allowed them to outlive the individual who contributed to their creation. The concept of the institution provided fertile ground for mutually supportive structures to arise; religion, law, government, education, genetic elitism. Eventually the dynamics of national cultures evolved. Now these cultures confront each other, vying for supremacy.

Today institutions are the hallmark of our culture. As we depend upon our culture to nurture us, so we depend upon our institutions for survival. For most of us this means working within a corporate institution of some sort; for those outside it means relying upon our institutions to secure the resources necessary to maintain us. Institutions of one sort or another also provide for our spiritual and emotional needs.

Institutions have lives of their own. They reproduce, they adapt and survive, they exchange energy and material with their environment; in fact, in many ways they can be regarded as life forms in their own right. A preposterous notion? Not really. True, they would be nothing but meaningless structures, inert materials and bureaucracy without humans. But is this not a fairly direct comparison with a human, if you could remove the genetic material from each cell? If you are just a modest 'cog in the wheels' of industry, government or whatever, are not your contributions to that institutional being similar to those of genes in an animate being?

And, as of mice and men, institutions develop their own morphologies. The shape, manifestation and results of an institutional existence are obvious. And the interaction between their morphologies is directly comparable to the interaction between that of various species of life. Some are compatible and mutually supportive: church and state. Others are complementary: property and law. And others are antagonistic, or relatively so: competing companies, religions or political ideologies.

As the world becomes more crowded, and those in nations with strong institutional morphologies pursue rising expectations, pressure is generated throughout the global system. In our society this is perceived as competition. We are all encouraged to believe in 'healthy competition', striving for a generalised notion of 'more'. The necessity of competition is a key assumption of our way of life, but since for those prone to heart conditions the effort of indulging in it is so often a fatally destructive activity, we should try to gain some insight into the real beneficiary of our competitive ethic.

From the time we enter school, and in many cases well before, we are set on the competitive path. Children are encouraged to labour alone on problems they could solve easily together. After climbing as high as they can up the academic tree, where those at the top will find themselves on very narrow isolated branches, they will leap into a career in an institution. Here the rules of engagement will be more complex; as well as advancing his own career, the young executive will also be subjected to the abrasive refining process of having to co-operate with those of equal rank. A high degree of stressful conformity is demanded. It is difficult to see how individuals in these circumstances can avoid being pushed onto the back slope of the human function curve, with the inevitable results of exhaustion and illness.

One way of looking at this is to regard it as an extension of the 'survival of the fittest' ethic. Although most scientists involved with questions of evolution reject this popularisation of Darwinian theory, it has nevertheless permeated the popular consciousness, and it has an element of truth. Predators do weed out the weakest or unluckiest, and the strongest males do tend to breed with higher-ranking females. But within the species there is little destruction of weaker members by stronger. Certainly, no species seems to delight in the destruction of its members as humans do.

Continuing conformity and competition, whether in a multinational company, the Church of England, or the Praesidium of the Soviet Union, is directed ultimately to the same end; the beneficial growth of the institution. The life of organisation man has been described as a rat race, but this is an oversimplification. It is more analogous to the ant or termite nest. The individual morphology of the average ant is very weak;

in isolation it dies. Each ant is better thought of as more like a cellular component of the nest; the merging of all their individual morphologies produces the viable morphology of the nest.

The analogy of ants in their nests and humans in their institutions is obvious, and it once more raises the question of our individuality. Those at high heart disease risk will be of two sorts; those type A organisation persons who have merged their selves to a very high degree with their institution, and those who are struggling to get into an institutional position that will nurture and protect them. The benefits to the individual of working inside an institution are bought at the price of submission to its more powerful nature.

Charles Erwin Wilson, a little-known American engineer industrialist, may have thought what was good for the country was good for General Motors and vice versa, but we need to question such wholehearted abrogation of self to institutional good. If what is good for General Motors and America is not good for you, it must be rejected.

It appears that human morphology does allow for a high degree of individuality. We thrive in small social groups which give us security and a high reflection of our individuality. But because of the impetus of our social evolution and the pressure developed by increasing human numbers we have been forced to evolve further. The institutional form of organisation, common to all advanced human societies, represents the way in which we are truly different from any other life forms. It is an expression of existence beyond our genes.

The institutional forms we have engendered now dominate our lives. We are confronted by institutions at every level of human need and interaction. The problems of dealing with faceless bureaucracies are well known, and the problems of exerting control over our environment through the mechanisms devised for the purpose are so helpless that a continual rash of *ad hoc* groups of 'concerned individuals' arises to battle with the monolithic nature of institutions pursuing institutional ends.

As we have presently arranged things in the developed industrial nations, our relationship with our organisational progeny is not proving too successful. Those intractable diseases of culture, including heart disease, may be finally laid at the door of the structure of our society. The question of the eradication of these diseases depends upon the degree to which we are able to organise our society and to which we have any choice in the larger questions which govern our lives.

Jonas Salk's observation, which we quoted earlier, is worth reconsidering in this context: 'We are participants in the evolutionary process: we are victims of the effects we cause.' If we accept this as literal truth, and there seems no reason to doubt it, then we are presented as a species with a stark choice. Either we modify our cultural forms of organisation and the structure of our society, thus recreating the possibility of more healthy individual life structures, or we continue with current trends, developing more ways of destroying ourselves.

For reasons which we have developed in detail in our book *Illness is Optional*, we believe that our alien observer of the human condition would come to a conclusion something like this: humanity has entered an arena of evolution which is qualitatively different from that of any other species. Because it is a product of our consciousness, we can choose our direction from that arena. It may be regarded as hopelessly idealistic to suggest that we should be able to choose the best of what we find before us, and to shed the harmful. But in the absence of such a conscious choice, our lives will increasingly be dominated, distorted and destroyed by the needs of our institutional creations.

It is possible for us to exert meaningful influence on human life structure, both at the individual level and at the level of our species. By becoming aware of the nature of human society, and the forces that we generate within that society, we have taken the first step in modifying those forces. The ultimate answer to the problem of heart disease has to do with the unconscious connection between individuals within a species. It has been described as 'morphic resonance', a term which explains how members of a species come to have shared knowledge and understanding. It is a force that unites humanity, underlining conformity within each particular culture.

If we in our human groups develop patterns of thought and behaviour that are bad for us as individuals, we will suffer. If such deleterious forces are incorporated into the institutionalised structure we have created, the society will suffer. One way such suffering will show is in epidemics of intractable disease.

The answer to what is at fault in our life structure lies in the way we think. If enough of us think in ways that are healthy for our species, healthy behaviour will follow. If the majority of us can be persuaded to do this, it will eventually affect all levels of our existence; we will devise the best exit from our current arena of evolution.

At the individual level we have to make a conscious decision about our priorities. The key choice is this: do we devote our energies to maintaining the integrity of our being and our personal morphology, or do we submit to the demands of our social structures, the higher morphologies of institutions, whatever the personal cost?

The change may have already begun with you, with the way in which you see your world, your thoughts, your behaviour. In wishing to live a better healthier life, you have no option but to make life itself better and healthier. Nothing can resist the power of an idea whose time has come.

CHAPTER 8

Strategies for Increasing Your Heart Life

Suit the action to the word,
the word to the action;
with this special observance,
that you o'erstep not the modesty of nature.

William Shakespeare *Hamlet*

This chapter suggests practical strategies for dealing with those things which put your heart at risk. The objective is to evolve a personal plan that gets you off the heart disease ladder, increases your health and promotes a happy and more fulfilling life. By following this plan, you should be able to create a way of life which avoids those disruptions of anticipation at the root of the problem. You should allow yourself a year to create effective change. Start with small steps that you know will be successful. Impossible goals are counter-productive; you need to build up momentum gradually in ways that are permanent.

We suggest that you use this chapter in the following way. Get yourself a large notebook, diary or loose-leaf folder. We will refer to this as your dossier. You will be using it to note information about yourself, to plan and record your progress. Date every entry. It will build up into your success story.

Start with your assessment of the current state of your health and fitness and the degree to which you are satisfied with your life, in the light of what you have learnt about heart disease. Set out your desires and goals for the future. You may change these as time goes by; that does not matter. It is always important to have clear goals to aim for.

Next set out your assessment scores. From chapter 3, your general heart disease risk – total A; your heart attack risk – total C (A+B scores); your protection level score – total P. From chapter 6, your main questionnaire score – total E; your D scale score – total D; and finally total F.

Leave columns so that when you reassess in the future you can record your new improved scores!

You will use these six total scores to work out your corrective strategy. The sections below are divided into three, corresponding roughly to the approach to the risk factors which we have followed in this book: 1) choices about what we consume, 2) life dynamics and 3) our life structure. Use your scores and your knowledge of your situation to identify your primary problem in each section. Three specific health problems – overweight, diabetes and hypertension – are discussed before section 1.

Note that if you had a high score for totals C, D, E or F, you should progress with special care so that you do not add to your stress-loading.

Be honest about your priorities. Only you will suffer from massaging or slanting your answers. Resist the temptation to avoid difficult areas. For instance, if you are a heavy smoker, but you do not care about meat and products high in animal fat, be aware that you might be tempted to rate 'animal fat' as your primary problem in section 1. Knowing you can solve this problem quickly and painlessly, you could give yourself an illusory glow of satisfaction – while ignoring a more important problem.

Do not be impatient. Remember – you have probably taken years to slip into your current state and there are no instant answers. But you can make a start. You should aim for regular but permanent improvements.

The secret is to make haste slowly. Reweave the fabric of your life to suit your heart's desires, without tearing it apart in the process. The more severe your risk and the older you are, the longer you will take to get clear and the more you need to be calm and determined.

Things to avoid: Do not join the therapy shoppers. If you have become newly aware of a risk of heart disease, do not panic. Rushing around trying first this cure, then another substance, therapy or approach in an incoherent way is more likely to precipitate problems than solve them. Do not allow yourself to be blinded by mystique.

Do not join the middle-age sports death statistics. Do not imagine that although you have not been physically active for many years, you are still coloured by the final flush of your youth. Men particularly are prone to rush off to prove themselves fit, and crash fatally in the process. Build up gradually.

Do not retreat into believing that altering one crucial thing in your life will make all the difference. It might make some difference but, if you ignore the others, this will not be enough. It is similar to the belief in 'the pill', or 'the operation'.

Avoid tokenism. If you find yourself 'doing your heart stuff' once a week and forgetting it for the rest of the time, you might as well forget it altogether. Not suffering from the epidemic means changing your life so that the problem does not arise for you.

Things to bear in mind: Living for any period of time in a way which encourages heart disease will mean that your body has developed coping or compensating mechanisms. No matter how harmful these mechanisms may be in themselves, you may not be able to remove them without putting something in their place. It is all too easy to substitute one harmful habit for another. Your aim should be to substitute something beneficial.

Restructure your metabolism and life to avoid the need for

harmful mechanisms. If the harmful mechanism was fulfilling a valid need, you have to work out how to fulfil that need beneficially.

Things that will help: Give yourself positive feedback. One way to do this is to use two colours for entries in your dossier. Pick a colour you like for targets, plans and positive results. Use a different one for episodes of backsliding. As you look back through the pages, you will be able to see how far you have progressed. When you are feeling good, you should look at your problem areas and periods when your behaviour did not meet expectations and see if you can work out what was going on.

If you are dealing with related problems in each section, your action on one will tend to make your actions on the others possible. For example, if you have tried to give up smoking, you will know how difficult this is in isolation. However, if at the same time you are altering your life dynamics to include increasing amounts of activity, you will find that the two do not mix. If your approach to your life structure changes so that your attitudes to the broader issues that encourage you to smoke are altered, giving up almost becomes automatic.

If the task ahead seems onerous, try writing down ten things which give you particular pleasure. Then, starting with number ten, plot them in along your projected course. When you achieve each objective – it might be your first day without sugar, or without cigarettes or the day you walk four miles in less than an hour – reward yourself. Do it! That way, determined effort and greater success lead to greater reward.

What follows are only suggestions. You may find them unsuitable for your situation, in which case your task is to devise variations that suit you better, while achieving the same ends.

Go on to section 1 if you are neither overweight, diabetic, nor hypertensive.

Overweight

I have more flesh than another man
and therefore more frailty
>Falstaff in Shakespeare's *Henry the Fourth*

If you are doubtful whether or not you are overweight, then you should not worry about it. Increasing your activity level should resolve any residual doubts. This section is for those who are sure that they are too fat.

There are two rules for dealing with fat:

1 Do not diet. Follow the general advice given on eating in this chapter.
2 Throw away your bathroom scales. You are not a sack of potatoes. The quality of flesh is what you are concerned with, not quantity.

When people lose weight by dieting, their bodies shed healthy lean tissue along with fat. When the unnatural regime breaks down, they cease to diet and put on more fat, but not more lean tissue. And so they proceed, losing vital tissue, including that of the heart, and replacing it with fat as they go up and down on the weight/diet seesaw.

What you eat is very important, how much you eat is largely irrelevant. Yet attempting to eat less is what the majority do. The failure of this strategy should be obvious; as a nation we are eating less, but getting fatter.

Obese people are unfortunate. Either they have been brought up as obese children by ignorant parents, a growing problem in Britain, or they are mature people who hate their bodies. For both the initial answer to the problem of their body lies in their heads. Counselling for confidence and self-acceptance may be the first step to positive change. We are back to questions of pleasure and guilt again; obese people need to unlock the door to the almost infinite sensual pleasure a fit and responsive body can provide.

To lose that unwanted fat, you need to make friends with your body, to understand why you choose to eat as you do. The fact that your concern has brought you this far is good, do not lose heart or courage. There are other books, that may help you go further, listed on p. 232.

In simple physical terms, fat accumulates when you do not use your muscles enough. When you are in harmony with your body, warts and all, and can get pleasure from it, start to use it more. Increasing your level of activity will burn off that fat. But the warning we gave earlier is particularly important to you: build up your activity level gradually. Remember that too much reabsorbed fat puts a strain on the system. You will lose it slowly at first, but the more you lose, the more you will be able to lose. You might find the 'dance' routine a good start.

If you are over thirty, or very fat, you cannot hurry fat loss without adding to your risk. But you will lose fat as your general condition improves. Be patient but persistent.

Diabetes

The majority of mature onset diabetics are overweight, and probably will have been so for some years. The section above probably applies to you if you are diabetic.

It is essential that you make a determined stand against heart disease. Your greatest risk comes from seeing yourself as an invalid and leaving it up to doctors to manage your condition. If you wish to avoid the conditioned patienthood that many encourage in diabetics, you must take control. You must play a dominant part.

You need to eat a very high fibre diet containing a large proportion of unrefined carbohydrates. The foods which have the most favourable metabolic profiles for blood sugar control are beans and oats. Starchy vegetables such as potatoes are also valuable. You should include as much wholemeal bread, wholewheat pasta, brown rice as you can in your diet, but add minimal quantities of fatty spreads and sauces. Your diet may have to be rather plain because you have to cut down on fats. Use spices and strongly-flavoured fruits and vegetables to provide flavour and variation. More information on diet is to be found in section 1.

You will have to learn by experience how these foods affect you. Every diabetic is different; for you, more than anyone else, 'know thyself' is the essential condition for health. This is especially important when you are increasing your level of activity.

Avoid hypoglycaemia by eating plenty of bulky carbohydrate foods in good time. If you use insulin, you have to keep rapid-acting carbohydrates available, but you should try not to need them. Dried fruit is preferable to glucose or other sweets to raise blood sugar in emergencies.

Physical activity will reduce your need for tablets or insulin. Regular activity helps to keep your blood sugar level stable and, more important, it will minimise those other long-term complications associated with the condition. You should aim to spend at least an hour a day in some form of aerobic activity. Start from where you are, and involve your doctor if it will give you more confidence.

Through a combination of prudent diet and aerobic activity, you should be able to reduce your weight to its ideal level. This may be enough to make your diabetes disappear completely, particularly if you developed the condition in middle age. But you will have to continue being very active all your life, or the problem will come back.

You will need to monitor your treatment and food needs very carefully. If possible, involve a friend or partner. Ask him or her to keep an eye on you when you walk or exercise: others can quite often pick up the signs of impending hypoglycaemia before the diabetic does. Signs include loss of healthy colour from the face, a complexion with a touch of yellow or grey; dark rings round the eyes and a baggy look beneath them; and increasing irritability. Partners of diabetics should bring these signs to the diabetic's attention. A hot cuppa and a sandwich will usually restore normality at this point. Attention to detail is important.

Hypertension

Hypertension can be partly due to inappropriate eating. Read section 1, pay special attention to sugar and the sodium potassium balance. Smoking makes the hazards of high blood pressure much more serious.

Activity: Regular aerobic activity will reduce blood pressure in the majority of hypertensives. Blood pressure rises with increased body fat. Activity keeps body fat down.

Stress and Exhaustion: Hypertension is a common result of working too near the limits of your capacity for too long. Pay particular attention to section 2.

Section 1

If your A Score was less than 5, you should go forward to section 2.

Eating: general considerations

The next four factors are concerned with specific aspects of the food we eat. Before looking at these, there are background considerations which apply to us all, whatever our particular dietary problem. Our eating habits are formed by many influences; what we are accustomed to, our upbringing, personal inclination and prejudice, ignorance and convenience. All have a background of cultural, social and commercial pressures. Paradoxically, in Britain we have a wide choice of foods from various other countries of the world, yet we persist in making unhealthy choices.

Family tradition may provide a rigid basis for our eating habits. Not only in terms of what we are accustomed to, but also because of the inertia of family eating. If one member wants to change, everyone may have to change. This can make it a lengthy process. Cooking habits and shopping routines have to be modified.

The best approach is to involve all the family in the planning stage. Discuss the reasons for change with those most resistant. If they object to your proposals, ask them to suggest equally desirable alternatives. The best solution is often to change one thing at a time, gradually shifting everybody's dietary base.

Single working people are probably influenced more by convenience. A token breakfast, the easiest lunch break and evening meal; a routine only modified by social occasions. A block approach may be the answer, first change your breakfast, then your lunch, and so on.

We often do not know what it is we are eating. Most packaged foods are notional concepts; the label may say beans in tomato sauce, but it will not say how much sugar, salt, colouring, preservative, conditioner, flavouring, inhibitors, pesticide residues and the myriad other additives you will get with your beans.

The only answer to this persistent health hazard is comprehensive food labelling. Grudging and belated improvements are on the way, but unless labelling is clear and comprehensive the contents of manufactured foods will always be suspect. Your voice added to the demand for this elementary right to know will help it to be achieved.

There are two general principles that you should always have in mind when choosing food:
1) Good food is food that will go bad – fresh food.
2) The best food is the least processed – natural food.

When buying fresh food do not be fooled by the packaging. According to Tony de Angelli on the Jimmy Young

Programme, 'It is the way that food is presented that makes it fresh in the consumer's eyes.' Mutton dressed up as lamb perhaps.

Remember, every time something is done to a food it is made less natural. Although a certain amount of cooking may be necessary, every process detracts in some way from the essential nature of the food.

Some foods have positive benefits to help you in your battle against heart disease. These are grains, seeds and fruits. Oatmeal porridge, eaten without sugar in the traditional Scottish way, is a delicious savoury dish, which is capable of reducing blood cholesterol levels. Eat your oats raw in muesli or baked into oatcakes, if you cannot cultivate a taste for porridge. Fresh or dried beans, peas and lentils offer similar benefits, and help to stabilise blood sugar levels. They make nourishing high-protein soups and main-course meals. Try to eat foods from this group every day. Complement them with wholewheat bread, pasta or rice. Finally, raw fruit and salads contain the vitamins and minerals you need to balance your system and help you to resist stress. Eat as much as you like.

Changing from a conventional Western diet to one rich in beans, whole grains and raw fruit and vegetables could have a laxative effect. Your gut will get used to the new regime quite quickly, and you will feel fitter and fresher. Don't worry about it. In the long term, this will benefit you, protecting you from certain cancers and bowel conditions as well as heart disease.

Sugar

Objective: To avoid all refined sugar.

Perspective: Britain consumes more sugar than any other nation, 3lbs (1½kgs) of sugar per person, on average, every week. It is frequently claimed that sugar is an essential part of the diet. In our view, refined sugar is totally unnecessary and has no place in any healthy diet. Professor Yudkin called it 'pure, white, and deadly'; we would remind you that it is potentially deadly, whatever its colour.

Action: Log your consumption of sugar each day and work at decreasing it. Monitor your progress and make sure you really are winning. Do not hide sugar in other foods, there are too many people doing that for you already.

Give up eating sweets, chocolate, sweet biscuits, puddings and cakes. Substitute fresh fruit or savoury snacks, if necessary. Then stop adding sugar to food and drink. If you cannot bear tea, for example, without sugar, you may need to stop drinking it till you have lost your sweet tooth. Before long, you will find that almost everything tastes better. Do not change to using artificial sweeteners: your aim is to lose the desire for the sickly excessive sweetness of modern food.

Moving away from processed and prepared food will help to cut down your consumption of hidden sugars. Read all labels carefully. Most tinned foods contain sugar; avoid these brands.

Effects of reducing refined sugar: You may feel the lack of that 'sugar rush'. Your body will quickly adjust and you will be out of the insulin rebound trap. Once you are running on longer-acting carbohydrates, you will notice that the short-term boost is replaced by deeper, more substantial energy reserves.

You may have to eat more. Do not worry about this: unrefined carbohydrates such as bread and potatoes are much bulkier than sugar, because they come complete with water and fibre in a total nourishing package. You would have to eat more than two pounds of apples to get a similar quantity of sugar to that in one Mars bar. And the sugar in apples is not hazardous at all.

Two bonuses may strengthen your resolve. When you cut out sugar, you may well lose weight. In addition, your skin will be clearer, your teeth will grow stronger and you will look generally healthier.

Dietary Fat

Objective: To reduce your intake of fat from food.

Perspective: Before 1850, our diet contained less than twenty-five per cent fat. Today, the average British diet delivers nearly fifty per cent of its energy value in the form of fats. This is excessive and dangerous. Reduction of saturated animal fat and cholesterol is most urgent, but a general reduction of dietary fat is desirable.

Action: Refer to tables 1 and 3 in chapter 9. Decrease your regular intake of high fat foods, and shift your diet as a whole towards the low fat foods.

Strategy: Many of us have little idea of what we actually eat in the course of a day or a week. Record everything you consume in your dossier, perhaps from the shopping list, until the pattern is clear. This will enable you to identify your main sources of dietary fat.

You should not try to cut fats out completely; they are essential to health. However, you could choose forms that will enhance your health rather than diminish it. This means replacing hard fats with cold-pressed oils wherever possible. Olive, sunflower, safflower and similar minimally processed oils are versatile and beneficial. Do not heat any oil more than once.

Do not butter your bread automatically: dry bread or toast is often fine with soup or other foods. Use little fat in preparation and cooking, and skim off meat dishes. Trim all visible fat from meat and choose the leanest cuts. Substitute fish for meat and dairy produce whenever possible.

Effects of reducing dietary fats: The attraction of fats is that they are generally rich high-energy foods. Cutting back on fats may mean that you will feel hungry, and have to eat more of other, bulkier foods. Listen to your body and go along with it. Treat yourself to a baked potato with pickles!

Once you have adjusted to the change you will feel more energetic. Animal fats demand a lot of processing energy from the body; your more healthy diet will release this capacity for more directly productive purposes. When your muscles are running on fat, they need extra oxygen; so if you have a heart problem, you will find that a less demanding food source could bring immediate benefits.

You may also lose weight, but do not count on it.

Dietary Salt

Objective: To lower sodium salt consumption, to increase potassium consumption and redress the dietary imbalance.

Salting was a preserving process developed to store foods over the winter in temperate climatic zones. Before that, we consumed relatively large quantities of salt from the wood ash of our cooking fires. We have got used to the taste of salted food.

Action: Stop adding salt to food and gradually reduce quantities used in cooking. Decrease consumption of processed food, increase intake of high potassium foods. Table 2 in chapter 9 gives details of sodium and potassium content of some common foods.

If you have high blood pressure, cut back on sodium as quickly as you can. Otherwise adjust at a more leisurely pace. Increased potassium intake should naturally follow a dietary shift away from processed food.

Effects of changing salt consumption: Reducing sodium intake can make some people feel a little flat. If you are very physically active and you sweat a lot, you may need your salt. A warning sign that you may be cutting the sodium back too fast is cramp, typically in the calf muscles of the foot. If you experience this, note the time and circumstances in your dossier and try drinking more water (not more tea, coffee or alcohol). Dehydration could be the cause. If it reoccurs despite increased drinking, keep your salt level constant for a few days. The problem will probably go away. If it persists, it may be necessary to increase your salt intake again and maintain it at a slightly higher level for a week or two. Then once more try reducing it.

Caffeine Addiction

Objective: To avoid the disruption caused by excessive use of caffeine. What is excessive consumption? The short answer is that it is subject to individual variability, but a cup of coffee in the morning and after dinner, with two or three cups of tea between should cause no problems.

Perspective: It is better to avoid the need for coffee. Excessive coffee drinking is characteristic of people living on the back slope of the human function curve. If you are drinking a lot of coffee, you should pay particular attention to stress in section 2.

Action: The best way to discover your degree of dependence on caffeine is to try twenty-four hours without. Some people notice remarkable effects; you may find you can relax and sleep in a way you thought impossible, you may feel calmer and more relaxed. Or you may suffer withdrawal symptoms similar to those involved in giving up smoking. On the other hand, you may not notice any difference; if so, you do not have a problem with caffeine.

Log your consumption of both tea and coffee in your dossier over a few days. If it exceeds six cups per day, try a day without. Use your dossier to achieve a planned cut back to a more reasonable level. Treat yourself to pure fruit juices, bottled water or herb tea instead. If you do have a coffee problem, you may be able to cut back to one cup a day when you really appreciate it. Go for quality and enjoy your decreased consumption.

Smoking
(5 cigarettes or more a day)

Objective: To be free of addiction to nicotine.

Perspective: Giving up smoking is probably the single largest step anyone can take to improve their general health. Before you give up you should organise your life so that you are able to take the strain of giving up. Make sure you are well rested and prepared. If the prospect of giving up horrifies you, you should go on to section 2 before you attempt to tackle nicotine addiction. Do not try to hate smoking. This will generate guilt. Admit that it can be a very pleasant thing and that it may actually have made it easier for you to cope. That is why so many people do it. But you can live without it.

Timescale: It takes seven to fourteen days for nicotine to be eliminated from your system. Your body will produce the demand reaction for a year or more after you stop. Do not give in to that sneaky feeling that the occasional cigarette is all right because you have given up. After five years your lungs and blood vessels should have largely recovered from the damage caused by smoking, but the risk of heart attack falls very quickly after giving up.

Action: There are two approaches to giving up smoking, the abrupt stop and the gradual cut-back. The gradual cut-back has the apparent advantage of allowing you to smoke while giving up; however, it usually fails. Smokers who adopt this strategy are probably kidding themselves and prolonging the agony.

The best answer is the abrupt halt. Some forward planning will help. Look ahead for a time slot in your life which you anticipate will be relatively stress-free, which contains no major upheavals that would make you want to smoke more.

Start logging the time and circumstances of each cigarette in your dossier. This will help you to observe your smoking pattern and enable you to identify sticking points and provocative situations.

When you identify smoking patterns, your task is to break them up so that you can drop the smoking part. Many people smoke when they talk on the telephone; a cigarette helps them cope with the anxiety that telephone conversations often engender. If you are one of those, you might work out a deep breathing/mental relaxation routine to use just before dialling, or before answering. Learn to calm your nerves without smoking. The after-dinner smoke has a long tradition; it may actually aid digestion. Changing your diet may help, or avoiding large set meals altogether for a short time might be an answer. The key is to disrupt the habit pattern around the act of smoking.

Think about the bad stages you are going to go through in breaking your addiction, so that they will not surprise and throw you. Explore all those corners of your mind where lingering thoughts or feelings could break your resolve. Nicotine is a subtle drug, it will have created many allies inside you; these will all be mobilised in its defence. You have to try to disarm them first. Build positive rewards into your programme, 'After two smoke-free days I shall ...' And so on.

You may find books on giving up are helpful; check your local library. You could also contact the anti-smoking group ASH and the Health Education Council for their information packs. Your GP may know of a local anti-smoking clinic or group.

Smoking is very often a social act, and social support is important in the struggle to break the addiction. See if you can persuade family members or friends to give up at the same time as you do. Support each other in your determination to give up. Swap hints for dealing with the craving.

Negative effects: You are likely to suffer all the effects of giving up a highly addictive tranquilliser; irritability, nervousness, anxiety. You may suffer giddy spells, dizziness, sweating, feelings of chill, weakness or lethargy. This is your body and mind trying to force you back to the drug. Understand and resist! When this phase has died down you are quite likely to put on weight – but rarely more than half a stone. Change your eating/activity habits if you are worried about growing fat.

Positive effects: You are likely to live longer, your blood pressure may go down, you will be much less likely to suffer from infections, especially colds and 'flu. Your nose and throat will be clearer, food will taste better – and so will you.

Remember: You will always be at risk from re-addiction to smoking.

Oral Contraceptives

Objective: To control fertility without inhibiting sexual activity. Long-term use of oral contraceptives undoubtedly raises the risk of heart disease. And Pill dangers rise sharply as women pass the age of thirty. The safest options are the cervical cap, diaphragm and sheath. Sterilization is another possibility. It is readily available privately, and can be arranged under the National Health Service. Ask one of the widely-advertised charities, your family planning clinic or your doctor about details.

Section 2

The strategies at this level are concerned with our interaction with the social and physical environment, the way we respond to options and the amount of control we have over the effects of our choices. We need to be alert to the almost infinite range of human variability. The blanket advice which was appropriate to issues like diet is not appropriate to these aspects of life. We cannot say precisely how much time you should have to yourself, how much you should weigh or how happy you should be.

You may notice such chicken-and-egg puzzles as, 'Do I like sweet things because I am unhappy, or am I unhappy because I eat too many sweet things?' It may help to ask yourself whether your behaviour in each area is freely chosen or imposed upon you. Do you do it because you want to, or because circumstances push you into it? If the former, you are in control. You can decide how much you want to continue adding to your risk. In the latter case, you must think carefully about the source of this loading. You will probably find links with other problem areas. For example, if you do not like your job, you may smoke to help you cope with it.

Remember: Heart disease is a product of a way of life. Altering your life dynamic is the way you avoid that product.

Activity

Study this section if your P score was under 20. Go on to Stress (p. 201) if your P score was 20 or more.
Caution: Do not do too much at first.

If you have been relatively inactive for some years, you will not know your capacity or your limits. You have got to find your way around your body again. Whatever you do, start by aiming to do half of what you think you are capable of and build up from there.

Even if you are active, you may be on a plateau of routine to which you are acclimatised. A different or more strenuous form of exercise could be dangerous. What we want is not specialist excellence, but a wide general capacity – a range of anticipatory capacity that life will not disrupt.

Use your knowledge of the human function curve to decide

when to exercise. When you are well rested, at the bottom of the front slope is best. Never exercise when you are tired or your body is telling you not to. And choose a time of day that suits you. Early morning running does not suit us, we like it better nearer midnight; it is a very personal thing.

The ground rules for healthy activity are these:

Extend your capacity by working within it. The natural processes of your body will give you more capacity when you are using what you have.

Work with your body; do not brutalise it or attempt to beat yourself into submission.

Do not try to break pain barriers.

Do not push yourself so hard that you have no breath left to talk – though a halting conversation is all right if you are working hard.

Do not exercise if you are feeling cold. Wrap up well and take layers off as you heat up. Exercise indoors in very cold weather.

Do not push yourself into strenuous activity if you are feeling upset or ill.

Avoid activity if you are running a temperature.

Avoid activity in the heat of the day in midsummer.

Always wear clothing, preferably cotton, that gives ample space for muscles to swell and allows for movement. Always have suitable footwear.

Make sure you warm up before strenuous activity. Suitable routines are given in *Physical Fitness* (see below) and other sources. Warming up means stretching and working the muscles you are going to need gently before you put any strain on them.

Give yourself plenty of time to recuperate and relax after a strenuous activity session.

Do not establish fixed or narrow routines of activity, remember the plateau problem, and a change can be better than a rest.

Take up a variety of different sorts of activity, building one type on another.

Use your increasing fitness to learn new sports or physical

pastimes – keep fit to enjoy more of life, not just to be fit.
You are never too old or too unfit to improve your fitness.
And enjoy your activity! Have fun! If you are gritting your teeth
and struggling miserably, consider a different form of activity –
or ask yourself where you picked up the idea that activity is
unpleasant. Are you burdened with damaging prejudices?

If anyone advises you against physical activity, there are two
things you should do. One, listen very carefully to what is being
said and judge its relevance to you. Ask questions and make sure
you get clear answers. Second, assess your adviser. Could this
person strip off and impress you with his physical condition?
Could he run a quick half mile to avoid trouble? Are his muscles
firm and useful? Is he cheerful, calm, confident? If not, you
should allow his condition to influence your opinion of his
opinions.

Individual Activities

If your P score was less than 10 or your C score over 180:
You need gentle, rhythmic activity to build up your stamina.
This sort of activity is suitable for people under stress; it will
refresh your body and calm your mind. For the absolutely
unfit beginner there is a 'dance' routine in chapter 9 which
makes a good start. After that the primary activity for you is
walking.

You should aim to go for a walk twice a day, building up speed
and distance over the course of weeks. See the section on
'walking' in chapter 9. All you need is a pair of shoes; you have
everything else you need.

Other suitable cardiovascular activities include swimming
and cycling. Again, build up speed and distance gradually. Do
not allow yourself to get cold. Reassess your P score monthly as
you build more activity into your life.

P score 10 to 20:
Go for a test walk of two miles (measured precisely on a map or

using a car mileometer). Go as briskly as you can, and if possible without stopping.

If your test walk is completed in less than thirty minutes, and you are not panting or in any pain, you should start running (see below for advice on getting started). Other suitable activities include cycling, swimming, weight training and dance.

If your test walk takes more than thirty minutes, or causes you any pain apart from slight stiffness in the calves, you should improve your condition through taking walks until you can achieve this basic level of performance.

Get a copy of *Physical Fitness* (Penguin, 1964). This book gives detailed instructions on the Royal Canadian Air Force programme for getting fit. The 5BX exercise plan for men is designed to take eleven minutes, while the XBX plan for women takes twelve minutes. No special equipment is needed. You work gradually through the exercises, fitting more and more into your eleven- or twelve-minute session. Finish off the session with a run outdoors, covering anywhere between one and six miles, according to the way you feel. In poor weather, running and jumping on the spot indoors is recommended. Full information is to be found in the book.

With this system it is particularly important that you do not try to prove your fitness on the first day; you could wake up like the proverbial board the next day! Follow the instructions carefully – and heed the warnings given.

Think about building more regular activity into your life. Walk or cycle to work. Avoid slipping behind the wheel every time you want to go somewhere. A good rough rule is 0–2 miles, walk; 1–5 miles, bike; 5 miles or over, drive if you must.

Stress: general considerations

This section should be read by all those whose E score was over 120, F score over 140, or D score over 10. The higher your E score, the more important this section is for you.

People respond to chronic stress by developing a range of

coping mechanisms. These may be reflected in high A and C scores. It is essential that you recognise these mechanisms for what they are.

You should not try to remove the mechanisms for coping with stress without removing the causes of stress. The physiology of stress is such that natural short-term protective mechanisms can become over-used and extended to the point of breakdown. Cutting off support in the form of coping behaviour could be like taking the lid off a pressure cooker without cooling it first.

Dealing with stress requires a continuing realistic appraisal of yourself and your situation. Logically removing a coping mechanism, no matter how understandable, will increase your stress. Dealing with a cause, no matter how difficult, will decrease it.

Stress generators are often buried deep, and to locate and come to terms with them will require diligence, persistence and imagination. You will need to build up your resources to tackle these problems. Take particular heed of Time and Exhaustion (see below).

The first requirement is better fitness, more physical resilience. Without this initial improvement you may not be able to cope with the stress of de-stressing yourself. There is no easy path; you have a battle on your hands, and you need to be fit for it.

This is not a new problem. Hippocrates developed a three-part regime for Greeks who had become overstressed by politics and mathematics. His approach would offer great benefits today. You might consider how you could set up your own equivalent. On the island of Cos, he had three stations. The first was a quiet place, where patients could sleep for as long as necessary. Then they would go to the second station, the beach. Here they would relax and play. Finally, after this convalescent stage, they would move to the gymnasium, where they would build up their physical strength and stamina. This gave them the capacity to deal with the problems which had previously defeated them.

Hippocrates realised that if you are highly stressed, you probably will not be in a fit state to tackle the things that cause it. Chronic stress affects different people in different ways, and can have many causes. Recall the definition given in chapter 5: the problem is that running your systems near the limits of their capacity for too long makes catastrophe more probable.

Marital tensions, dissatisfaction at work and similar situations may not be resolved without a painful and perhaps dangerous crisis. Problems of this sort often grow steadily worse because those involved find it so difficult to confront the issues. Years of bitterness may come to a head.

Many people unfortunately suffer emotional crises when they stop banging their heads against walls. Others seek high stress situations because they are stimulating and attractive, much as the moth is drawn to the flame.

Even if you feel your stress level is manageable now, remember that stress has a cumulative effect over time. Improving your condition will give some leeway, but you need to get yourself on the front slope of that human function curve before the need is forced upon you. It is much more difficult to improve your physical condition when you are suffering from any form of stress.

Learning relaxation techniques or taking up meditation will increase your resilience and help prevent much stress-induced damage. Transcendental meditation has been demonstrated to produce reliable health benefits and you should be able to find a class in your local area.

Emotional Stress

Tracking less obvious sources of emotional stress can be tricky. We are frequently our own worst enemies, burying the causes of our problems in order to avoid facing them. It is a common strategy to suppress knowledge so deeply within us that we can deny its existence. Denial does not make a stress generator go away. At best it will inhibit our choices of behaviour, at worst it will simmer away inside until a last straw provokes a breakdown. Such breakdowns can also manifest themselves in physical symptoms; hypertensives are frequently suffering from emotional stress.

The exploration of the deep causes of such stress may be difficult without skilled professional help. Venturing into the deep currents within us can be dangerous, and should not be attempted alone. A guide who can throw a life line should go with you. First-step counselling agencies are given on p. 233.

Emotional crises can actually set off heart problems. Disturbances of heart rhythm can accompany attacks of panic and our response to panic can make them worse. Overbreathing (p. 72) is usually a response to anxiety. It upsets the chemical balance of the blood and can set off a racing and irregular heartbeat, a condition familiar to many as 'palpitations'.

You will probably benefit from joining a yoga class and learning breathing exercises. This problem often stems from a breathing rate that is just marginally too high, continued over a long time. You may well have got into the habit of breathing in a way that is making you ill. The first step towards overcoming the problem is recognition of it; the next is to assert control over your breathing. Try to breathe from the abdomen, as a baby does. If you feel short of breath, remember that what you need is to use each breath more fully rather than to breathe more. Breathe slowly, counting up to four with each breath: in – two – three – four; out – two – three – four. This can be helpful during exercise too; we find it aids stamina when running.

If your life structure generates continual emotional stress, there may be no alternative to radical change. This will involve reconsidering your basic attitudes, assumptions and behaviour. You will need to be adventurous to break out of the mould that is damaging you.

A counsellor or therapist, even a good friend who can offer objective advice and listen with sensitivity, can often help you to understand how you cling to damaging situations. Emotional stress is so common that a great range of therapies are commercially available. We would not comment on these; their effectiveness depends very much on the beliefs you bring to them. If they work for you, fine.

If you do not have faith in anyone you know, you could try being your own counsellor. Explore your feelings on paper, writing down major sources of stress and unhappiness, looking for their roots and links with other features of your life. If writing does not come easily, tell your problems to a tape recorder. Bear in mind that we often think we cannot change things that in fact we can control; question your assumptions continually. When you have poured out your woes and explored all the avenues you have the energy to investigate, take a break of at least one day. Then read what you wrote or listen to your tape as critically and objectively as you can. Question it. Ask yourself whether there is something there that you have been refusing to face.

Writing down your problems helps you to put them in perspective. Just thinking about them can send you round in circles, achieving nothing. To be free of them you must break out of this pattern.

Emotional stress due to relationship problems often produces uncertainty about one's personal worth and social acceptability. Remember that you need not be perfect, nor should you expect yourself to be. Nor will you be universally liked or respected. Be true to yourself. If others, even important others, do not like this, you have to be able to shrug your shoulders. Your failings will be balanced by unique qualities, and everybody's taste differs. You may decide that your strategy will be to initiate an active search for people to whom you can relate without pretence.

You must insist that you be accepted for yourself. If the thought of being unashamedly assertive terrifies you, you should consider taking an assertiveness course. Everyone should have a justifiable pride in themselves; without this emotional integrity is very difficult. A psychologist should be able to help.

Personality and Behavioural Stress

If your E score was over 200, then this section is very important for you. If it was between 100 and 200, you should judge for yourself how far it applies to you: some parts will be relevant, others may not.

A high E score means that you show many characteristics of the type A personality, and that this type of behaviour is putting you at risk of heart attack. These are the questions you must answer:

Should you not put more of your energy into protecting your investment in yourself and your family?

Is what you are achieving really worth the risk entailed?

Is it true that you cannot change your life to avoid serious health risk?

How much longer can you expect your system to stand up to the level of damage you put on yourself?

A low C score does not give safety. Your risk is lower, but the super-fit still do have heart attacks if they subject themselves to the concentrated stress of type A behaviour. Leonard Rossiter was also a champion squash player, Jim Fixx a long-distance runner, but both died of heart attacks. Both demanded a great deal of themselves.

The essential change for you is in attitude. You have to put yourself and your emotional and social needs before the requirements of work, duty and achievement. You must refrain from sacrificing yourself for status or money. One-dimensional competitiveness must be exchanged for a fuller, more rounded life.

You should try to build up the things in your life that do not demand struggle, though they may have the challenge of requiring time and attention. If you live alone, find another being with whom you can share energy. If you do not like people, why not try a dog or a cat? Stroking animals has been found to reduce blood pressure; pet owners are less likely to have heart attacks and recover more quickly from major illness.

If you are this type of personality, you will find it difficult to change. To avoid the risk of heart attack, your most effective strategy must be to learn to live within your capacity. See Time and Exhaustion, below.

Time

For too many people time is a rare and elusive commodity. People who have heart attacks have often made an enemy of time, always working against it, allowing it to be used against them and abusing it, claiming they have no time to take action to improve their health. For most people the key to the problem is to become selfish. You must take the time you need.

Planning is essential. Use your dossier as a diary to plan ahead. Note where your time goes now, then begin to rearrange this structure. Book blocks of time with 'ME' written emphatically across them. Rearrange the other things around yourself. Everyone should aim to have at least one hour each day which is entirely their own. Not that tired time before bed when you are not up to much, but prime time when you could decide to do anything or nothing with no intrusions.

This requires single-minded determination. Too often our lives develop into a mesh of things we 'must' or 'ought' to do because of our interactions with others. The illusion of required standards and necessities can reach the point where we are trapped.

In promoting your health, time is essential. You must have command of it. Learn to manage it to achieve your ends. Stating these ends in your dossier should help to focus your need for your own time.

Take it!

Exhaustion

Living in a state of unrecognised or unacknowledged exhaustion is a major problem for people at risk of a coronary episode.

Sleeplessness is a symptom of over-running systems that will contribute to a state of chronic exhaustion. Exhausted people have pushed themselves beyond the point where their systems can achieve a balanced shut down for a recuperative night's sleep.

It is important to discriminate between healthy fatigue and exhaustion. The first is the normal effect of working on the front slope of your human function curve; the second drives you down the back slope. Acceptable fatigue is tiredness that you do not deny. You take steps to recover as soon as possible, and you are able to sleep when you get the opportunity.

A state of exhaustion means that you have to make large efforts to achieve quite limited goals. Your effectiveness falls short of what you expect. You become hot and bothered about things that would not normally upset you. You do not think as quickly and clearly as you should. You are slow off the mark, you fumble and lose your place. You feel resentful and are readily roused to anger. Your judgement declines. You are less able to separate important from trivial matters. You tend to indulge in displacement activities, such as eating, drinking, smoking and talking, rather than getting on with things.

To deal with exhaustion, you first have to make sure you can sleep. Inability to sleep soundly may be associated with excessive consumption of caffeine. Check this out.

Sleeplessness is such a common problem that there are many strategies for dealing with it. It may be a matter of minor personal routine; perhaps a hot drink or a book at bedtime, or a gentle stroll. Our dog is an invaluable aid in this; she will insist on her nightly tour of the neighbourhood.

If your problem is made worse by light, noise or people, do not procrastinate; take action. Turn it off, out or make it go away. Invest in comfortable earplugs, heavy lined curtains, or sound-proofing. The improvement can be tremendous.

Medicines will not offer more than a short-term answer. A wee dram of good whisky has much to recommend it, but larger quantities will interfere with sleep. Sleeplessness that follows relinquishment of tranquillisers or sleeping tablets will resolve itself in due course.

For long-term heart life the most effective action against bouts of sleeplessness is to redress the underlying imbalance. If the cause is not apparent, use your dossier to note events of the day; see if you can spot those things which wind you up, and set about correcting it. Anxiety may be a prominent feature. If you cannot solve the cause by discussion or rationalisation, you may be able to remove the effects. Physical exertion changes the state of the brain chemistry, as well as affecting the body.

Relationship problems or emotional disturbances are also common contributors to the problem. You may be able to resolve these by working together, perhaps with a counsellor, to achieve a satisfactory state. But you may have to end the liaison and start again. Lingering on in a half-life of conflict and unsatisfactory compromise can be intensely destructive in every sense.

Chronic pain may result in an inability to sleep. A higher level of physical activity is likely to be part of the answer and a deep relaxation technique such as meditation or breathing will help.

Chronic exhaustion may be a result of any of these situations remaining unresolved over a period of time. It may help to take some time off, perhaps a weekend away, to look objectively at your situation.

If your work is a major contributor to a state of chronic exhaustion, you have to make a difficult decision. If you cannot adjust, you must seriously consider the health cost of your job. Avoiding disease may require radical action. Is your job worth dying for? This is the bottom line question. Before reaching the answer, you have to consider a welter of conflicting forces, needs and assumptions.

It might be worthwhile to draw up a balance sheet. On one side list the benefits and advantages your job provides; on the other the costs and disadvantages. Evaluating the columns in terms of your life as a whole will be a very personal matter, but whatever you do, do not omit the bottom line question. A tangential question might help: 'If I were not going to work, living this way, what would I do?' Think again about the content of chapter 7, and move on to section 3.

Depression

Read this section if your D score was 10 or more or if you know you are prone to depression, even if you are fine just now.

When you are depressed, any illness has a better chance of taking you over. Conversely, depression often accompanies illness, and can follow infectious diseases such as 'flu. The usual medical answer to depression is to prescribe drugs which mask it. This helps little in the long term and may not even work for you in the short term.

Depression develops when our social and psychological needs are not being met. Having control over your life will help you avoid it, but there may be times when you just have to weather it, allowing your natural processes to recover. You may want to withdraw completely from the world. Go with that feeling, but do not make drastic decisions based on it: it is a temporary phase when withdrawal allows you to gather your internal resources so that you can take effective action to remedy the problems in your life.

Frustrated rage can be experienced as depression, particularly if you are the sort of person who finds it difficult to express anger. If your marriage or your job is draining more from you than you are getting out of it, your depression may mask fury with those who are damaging you. This is a possibility that is sometimes very hard to face, and depression can be a strategy of avoidance. You need a withdrawal period to come to terms with what is going on in your life.

Never allow yourself to imagine that your depression is meaningless, inexplicable. Do not waste this crisis: it happens for a good reason. Long-term depression may require a psychologist or counsellor to help you work out how to remedy the problem.

Short-term depression can sometimes be averted with prepared escape plans. A special treat, a visit to a friend, something to disrupt the pattern that is disrupting you. Backstops are also a good idea; what they are will depend on your temperament: a brisk bike ride, an hour in the jacuzzi with good blues music, whatever will turn you back. If you are exhausted all tactical manoeuvring is likely to fail; save it until you have slept it off.

Section 3

The connection between the larger components of life and questions of individual heart health is more elusive. Prescriptive detail becomes less possible. But these components do have effects and it is important to consider them.

Human culture can be considered as a living thing, a constantly changing process of exchange of varying input and output, action and reaction. As generators of culture, we are both initiators and recipients of its products. The plight of human affairs gives widespread cause for concern. The bad effects we generate, for ourselves and for our environment, seem to develop a momentum which takes them far beyond our individual control. And the institutions of our society appear to aid and abet this trend, against any notion of general welfare.

The tortuous governmental wrestling with the ethical problems of tobacco advertising is perhaps the most visible example. There are many others, including the high pressure marketing of products, which, if not bad for us, certainly keep their benefits well hidden. Healthy business corporations do not necessarily mean healthy consumers.

Just as individuals will believe things are right because they do them, so cultural entities will have effects which we accept and protect because they are part of our culture. As we need to question individual assumptions that are harmful, we also need to question cultural assumptions. The need is especially urgent when they produce disease epidemics.

In chapter 7 we outlined elements of life structure which we believe to be important common underlying threads of our species, the things which are applicable to us all by virtue of being human. Using this knowledge, applying it to yourself for positive effect, is a matter of attitude, your habitual way of regarding things. What we are going to suggest is general outlines of attitudes you should foster as a significant part of your health promotion. In changing your attitudes, we believe you will not only be helping yourself, but others as well.

The key attitude is an appreciation of life. To appreciate life you must first appreciate yourself. Start with understanding the way humans are intended to function; retrace the wonder of our species as marvellously developed and integrated beings. Too often we allow our command of technology and our institutional provisions to divorce us from the essence of the nature we have inherited from our evolutionary past.

The mass of men, according to Henry David Thoreau, lead lives of quiet desperation. If this was true at the time he made the observation – in late-nineteenth-century America amid pioneering goldrush adventure and wealth-building enterprise – how much more so today when the world is smaller and opportunities of all sorts diminishing? We have traded our freedom to explore and to risk for material consumerism and increased human numbers. Under the impotence of our life structure we settle for second-hand living through TV and video, and maintain what George Orwell described as 'a world safe for little fat men'. A world which is safe for heart disease would be another way of looking at it.

To be healthy we have ultimately to be a part of a balance of all life. In this sense the needs of the person are the needs of the planet.

Much of our social effort is directed towards removing the limitations that nature may impose upon us; in doing so we unavoidably destroy those elements of nature which thwart us, and much which is purely incidental; any notion of balance in our existence is extremely tenuous. Our nature expects us to live in a world we evolved to fit. While our physiology and much of our instinctive response lingers in expectation of these conditions, our consciousness and intellectual progress have extended us forward into a world of our own creation.

We need to adopt a totally different view of the future of humanity. New assumptions must guide our lives; we require a conceptual shift throughout our species. The objective is to weave in threads of a counter-culture that has human health as a dominant characteristic. We cannot continue indefinitely down the road of mass drug dependence and surgical replacement; the philosophy behind those approaches is simply wrong.

Is such a shift possible? There are signs that we are on the move. Books of esoteric philosophy dealing with such questions, which a few years ago would have had difficulty finding a publisher, now sell in respectable numbers throughout the world. Medicine is undergoing a revolution, with an upsurge of interest in holistic health and alternative therapies. There is a new concern with questions of the quality of life, and the influence we can have upon it.

The desire in such trends is for human scale, for a world amenable to our desires, for knowledge of ourselves in relation to that world. Ernest Schumacher summed much of this up in *Small is Beautiful*. Its relevance to health may not be immediately clear; small must equal personal, and the beauty be in a world constructed on human scale, designed as if people mattered.

We have been at pains to illustrate that heart disease is a multi-causal problem, rooted firmly in elements of our culture. The mechanistic causes, such as smoking and inactivity, and the lifestyle factors which lead to excessive stress, are easy to identify within our culture. The disparity of their effects is however harder to explain; on the one hand we have individual variability, and on the other we have the distortion of our culture, giving the disease its dynamic properties. Human activity generates forces which produce this distortion, compressing our basic culture and changing its shape. As components of our culture, we are in turn distorted.

We can change the shape of our existence from the largest to the smallest detail by the way we think and feel. In a very real sense we are all connected; if we share common desires and beliefs, there will be fulfilment of the content of those desires and beliefs. The predominant notions will resonate through our species and surface in the reality we create.

If you think and behave in ways which promote the health of your heart, you will be spreading the positive message. If enough people do the same, the epidemic of disease will disappear as mysteriously as it arrived. The conditions which nurtured it within our culture will have been eradicated. Our culture arises within you and it is there that the most profound changes must occur.

> No man is an island, entire of itself;
> every man is a piece of the Continent,
> a part of the main.
>
> Any man's death diminishes me,
> because I am involved in Mankind;
> And therefore never send to know for
> whom the bell tolls, it tolls for thee.

John Donne *Devotions*

CHAPTER 9

Reference Tables and Resource Guide

Diet

Table 1   Cholesterol Content of Foods

(Milligrams per 100 grams of edible parts)

Bacon, fried	80	Liver (calf)	330
Beef, cooked	80	Margarine (vegetable)	0
Brains (all kinds)	2200	Milk (whole)	14
Butter	230	Milk (skimmed)	3
Cheese (cheddar)	70	Oils (vegetable)	0
Cheese (cottage)	15	Oysters	50
Chicken (flesh)	60	Pork	110
Chicken (skin)	230	Salmon (canned)	90
Crab	100	Shrimp	200
Egg (whole)	450	Tuna (canned in oil)	70
Fish (fresh)	70	Sweetbreads	250
Ice cream (dairy)	21	Turkey	75
Kidney	400	Veal	90
Lamb	110	Venison	110
Lard or dripping	65	Yoghurt (low fat)	7

Table 2   Sodium and Potassium Content of Common Foods

(Mg per ounce *Na* = Sodium   *K* = Potassium)

	Na	K		Na	K
Cereal/Flour products:			*Fruit:*		
Digestive biscuits	124	44	Apples	.5	27
Wholemeal bread	132	74	Bananas	.3	99
White bread	146	30	Currants (dried)	5	201
Ryvita	175	133	Dates	1	215
Cornflakes	298	32	Figs (dried)	25	288
Porridge	164	12	Grapes (black)	.5	90
Weetabix	90	97	Melon (Cantaloupe)	4	90
			Orange	.8	56
Dairy produce:			Peach (fresh)	.8	74
Cheese (cheddar)	174	33	Peach (canned)	.4	43
Cheese (Danish blue)	402	53	Pears (fresh)	.7	36
Milk (fresh)	14	46			
Eggs (fresh)	38	39	*Vegetables:*		
			Beans (baked)	150	90
Meat:			Butter beans (boiled)	5	113
Bacon (fried)	880	140	Runner beans (boiled)	1	25
Beef (corned)	392	33	Beetroot (boiled)	18	99
Beef (roast)	20	101	Brussels sprouts		
Chicken (roast)	23	101	(boiled)	2	70
Ham (boiled)	595	129	Cabbage (boiled)	4	41
Pork (roast)	19	88	Carrots (raw)	27	64
Sausage (pork, fried)	284	58	Carrots (boiled)	14	25
			Leeks (boiled)	2	79
Fish:			Mushrooms (fried)	3	161
Cod (grilled)	31	116	Peas (boiled)	0	49
Herring (fried in			Peas (canned)	74	57
oatmeal)	29	118	Potatoes (boiled)	1	92
Kipper (baked)	281	148	(baked in skin)	2	193
Pilchards (canned)	169	87	Tomatoes (raw)	1	82
Salmon (steamed)	25	77			
Salmon (canned)	152	91	*Condiments:*		
			Table salt	11,000	0
Nuts:			Baking powder	3,350	14
Almonds (fresh)	1.6	243	Salad cream	238	22
Peanuts (fresh)	1.6	193	Tomato ketchup	316	168

Table 3 *Fat Content of Common Foods*

(per cent by weight)

Bread, cereals	2	Lamb chop (grilled, lean)	17
Fried bread	37	Lamb chop (fried)	60
Butter, margarine	85	Pork (roast, lean only)	20
Cheese (Camembert)	23	Cod (steamed)	1
Cheese (Cheddar)	35	Cod (fried)	5
Cheese (Edam)	23	Herring (fried)	13
Cheese (Stilton)	40	Salmon (canned)	6
Milk (whole)	3.7	Fruit and vegetables, fresh,	
Milk (skimmed)	.2	baked, or boiled (except	
Eggs (whole)	12	olives, avocado)	9
Bacon (fried back)	53	Almonds	54
Beef (corned)	15	Peanuts	49
Beef (roast, lean only)	15	Pastry	33
Beef steak (grilled)	22	Sponge sandwich cake	25
Chicken (roast)	7	Sweet biscuits	9

Drugs

(Names and recognised side-effects of common types used for heart disease)

The reality of drug testing, assessment, approval and monitoring in use is of necessity characterised by a degree of chance. There is always a possibility that a drug will be found to have new side effects and we cannot accept any responsibility for this.

Each drug has three different names, and the same basic drug is often available in a variety of forms. In the lists below, we give *generic*, or official names, and *brand names*, which are names used by particular manufacturers. Because different manufacturers can produce the same drug under different brand names, there are more brands than drugs.

Drugs are promoted under brand names, and these are the names you are likely to find on your prescription.

The list of side-effects cannot include all those that have been linked with each type of drug, and undoubtedly there are many that have not yet been recognised. If you think you may be suffering from a side-effect that is not mentioned here, look for more detailed information. The best source is *Martindale: The Extra Pharmacopoeia*, which can be found in good libraries. Other more accessible books are listed under recommended books (p. 232). Your pharmacist may be willing to help you, and some hospitals have drug information services. Naturally, you should discuss any suspected drug problem with your doctor – but be prepared for the possibility that doctors will deny that you are experiencing any drug-induced disease, even if they cannot be sure of this.

Beta-blockers

Brand names: Angilol, Apsolol, Apsolox, Bedranol, Berkolol, Beta-Cardone, Betaloc, Betim, Blocadren, Corgard, Inderal, Kerlone, Laracor, Lopresor, Sectral, Slow-Pren, Slow-Trasicor, Sotacor, Tenormin, Trandate, Trasicor, Visken.
Generic names: acebutolol, atenolol, betaxolol, labetalol, metoprolol, nadolol, oxprenolol, pindolol, propranolol, sotalol, timolol. Probably any drug name ending in 'lol'.

The following preparations contain beta-blockers in combination with a drug which increases urination – a *diuretic*. These products have the characteristics of beta-blockers and diuretics (discussed below): Co-Betaloc, Corgaretic, Inderetic, Inderex, Lasipressin, Lopresoretic, Moducren, Prestim, Secadrex, Sotazide, Spiroprop, Tenoret 50, Tenoretic, Tolerzide, Trasidrex, Viskaldrix.

These drugs block the effects of adrenalin on nerves which stimulate the heart, blood vessels, bronchi and liver. This reduces the strain on the heart and cuts its oxygen demand.

Side-effects of beta-blockers include excessive slowing of the heart, which can lead to heart failure; cold hands and feet; asthma; leg pain (intermittent claudication); diabetes. Beta-blockers make it difficult for diabetics to detect early signs of hypoglycaemia. Sleep disturbance, nightmares, depression, tiredness, weakness, dry eyes, headache and skin rashes can occur. Effects on the digestive system may include stomach pain, nausea and vomiting.

Diuretics

Brand names: Aldactide#, Aldactone*, Aluzine, Amilco#, Aprinox, Arelix, Baycaron, Berkozide, Brinaldix K, Burinex, Burinex K, Centyl, Centyl-K, Diamox, Diatensec*, Direma, Diumide-K, Diuresal, Diurexan, Dryptal, Dyazide#, Dytac*, Dytide#, Edecrin, Enduron, Esidrex, Esidrex K, Frumil#, Frusene#, Frusetic, Frusid, Hydrenox, HydroSaluric, Hygroton, Hygroton K, Kalspare#, Lasikal, Lasilactone#, Lasix, Lasix + K, Metenix, Metopirone, Midamor*, Moduret 25#, Moduretic#, Natrilix, Navidrex, Navidrex-K, Neo-NaClex, Neo-NaClex-K, Nephril, Saluric, Spiroctan*, Urizide.
Generic names: amiloride hydrochloride*, bendrofluazide, bumetanide, chlorothiazide, chlorthalidone, clopamide, cyclopenthiazide, ethacrynic acid, frusemide, hydrochlorothiazide, hydroflumethiazide, indapamide, mefruside, methyclothiazide, metolazone, piretanide, polythiazide, potassium canrenoate*, spironolactone*, triamterene*, xipamide.

Products marked * are potassium sparing diuretics (see below p. 220). Those marked # are compound preparations of two types of diuretic.

See also beta-blocker/diuretic combination list above.

Diuretics are drugs which cause increased production of urine. All but those marked * or # cause increased excretion of potassium. Consequences include disturbance of heart-beat, increased toxicity of other drugs, muscle weakness, constipation, loss of appetite and aggravation of diabetes.

Potassium supplements may be given separately. Brand names include Kay-Cee-L, K-Contin, Kloref, Leo K, Nu-K, Sando-K, and Slow-K.

Brinaldix K, Burinex K, Centyl K, Diumide K Continus, Esidrex K, Hygroton K, Lasikal, Lasix + K, Navidrex K, Neo–NaClex K are combination products containing a diuretic and potassium.

Warning: Never take any potassium supplement, alone or in combination, if you are taking a diuretic marked * or # in the lists above.

Diuretics can cause excessive diuresis, leading to depletion of blood volume, dangerously low blood pressure, and sometimes death. They may precipitate the onset of diabetes and make established diabetes worse. They commonly cause gout. They are also capable of causing nausea, dizziness, weakness, numbness, pins and needles, skin rashes and excessive sensitivity to sunlight, blood disorders, damage to the liver and pancreas, allergic reactions and impotence. Potassium sparing diuretics (marked * and # above) can, in addition, cause gastrointestinal disturbances, breast enlargement in men, drowsiness, headache and mental confusion.

Antihypertensives

Drugs in this group are rarely the first choice measures used for high blood pressure. They are more likely to be given at the same time as a beta-blocker or diuretic. Sometimes they form part of a cocktail of three, four or even more drugs. The risk of serious drug-induced disease rises with the number of products taken.

Any drug prescribed for high blood pressure may have an excessive effect, leading to a precipitous fall in blood pressure. This most often happens when the individual stands up, and it can result in falls and fainting, with consequences that can be serious, especially in the elderly.

Different types of antihypertensive drugs have a range of other adverse effects, some of which are listed below.

Vasodilators

Brand names: Apresoline, Eudemine, Hypovase, Loniten, Nipride.
Generic names: diazoxide, hydralazine, minoxidil, prazosin, sodium nitroprusside.
Adverse effects of the drugs listed above include fluid retention, tachycardia (fast heart-beat), weight gain, nausea and vomiting. Angina may be aggravated. Hydralazine (Apresoline) is also associated with a form of *systemic lupus erythematosus*, which is a disease akin to acute rheumatoid arthritis.

Centrally Acting Antihypertensives

1   *Brand names:* Aldomet, Dopamet, Hydromet, Medomet.
Generic name: methyldopa.

Methyldopa has over a hundred known adverse effects, affecting all body systems. Serious hazards include anaemia and other blood disorders and liver damage. Other side effects are impotence, sedation, drowsiness, depression, nightmares, nausea, dry mouth, stuffy nose, stomach upsets, diarrhoea, constipation, fever, dizziness and lightheadedness. It may also cause skin rashes, weakness, joint pain, and it can aggravate angina.

   If you are taking methyldopa and you suspect that you could be suffering from a different side-effect, we would advise that you consult the US publication, *Physicians Desk Reference*, or *Martindale: The Extra Pharmacopoeia*. Most other sources will not carry sufficient information on this drug.

2   *Brand name:* Catapres.
Generic name: clonidine hydrochloride.

Clonidine reduces arousal. When this goes further than desired, the drug is said to cause drowsiness. Most side-effects of clonidine are associated with its actions on the brain: dizziness, depression, headache, insomnia, nausea and euphoria. When long-term therapy is suddenly discontinued, the opposite effects – agitation and dangerously high blood pressure – can result. Other hazards include fluid retention, excessively slow heart-beat, and spasm of the arteries feeding the hands and feet, producing effects like chilblains.

3 *Brand names:* Abicol, Decaserpyl, Enduronyl, Harmonyl, Hypercal, Rautrax, Rauwiloid, Serpasil.
Generic name: reserpine.

These drugs can cause deep depression and are believed to be responsible for many suicides. For this reason, they have largely fallen out of favour. Other adverse effects are similar to clonidine, above (2). Reserpine has been linked with an increased risk of breast cancer.

Adrenergic Nerve Blockers

Brand names: Declinax, Esbatal, Ismelin.
Generic names: bethanidine sulphate, debrisoquine, guanethidine monosulphate.

These drugs have largely fallen out of favour because they produce faintness on rising, while they are not effective for the control of blood pressure when the patient is lying down. Their side effects include diarrhoea, cheek pain, muscle weakness, aggravation of intermittent claudication and failure of ejaculation.

Alpha-blocking Drugs

Brand names: Baratol, Dibenyline.
Generic names: indoramin, phenoxybenzamine hydrochloride.

These drugs can cause sedation, depression, dizziness, failure of ejaculation, dry mouth, nasal congestion and faintness on standing up. Dibenyline also causes rapid heart-beat (tachycardia).

Enzyme Inhibitors

Brand names: Capoten, Acepril.
Generic name: captopril.

Captopril can affect the bone marrow, reducing resistance to infection. If you are taking this drug and you develop any symptoms of infection (e.g. sore throat, fever), *you must consult your doctor without delay*, so that your white cell count can be checked.

This drug tends to raise potassium levels and must never be taken with a potassium sparing diuretic (marked * or # in the list above, p. 219) or with a potassium supplement (p. 220).

Other potentially serious reactions are skin disease and kidney damage. Side-effects include loss of taste, mouth inflammation, abdominal pain and dizziness.

Cardiac Glycosides

Brand names: Cedilanid, Digitaline Nativelle, Lanitop, Lanoxin, Ouabaine Arnaud.
Generic names: digoxin, deslanoside, digitoxin, lanatoside C, medigoxin, ouabain.

These drugs are poisonous if you take a little too much. Because of the variation between individuals, the dosage is very difficult to judge and poisoning is common. Symptoms include nausea, excessive salivation, vomiting, loss of appetite, diarrhoea, abdominal pain, headache, pain in the face, drowsiness, depression, malaise, disorientation, delirium, mental confusion, pins and needles, blurred vision, distorted colour vision, extra heart-beats and disturbances of heart rhythm and, finally, heart failure.

Vasodilators

Vasodilators used for angina

Brand names: Adalat*, Cardiacap, Cedocard, Clinium, Cordilox*, Coro-Nitro Spray, Elantan, GTN 300, Ismo 20, Isoket, Isordil, Monit, Mono-Cedocard, Mycardol, Natirose, Nitrocine, Nitro contin, Nitrolingual Spray, Pentoxylon, Percutol, Peritrate, Pexid, Securon*, Soni-Slo, Sorbichew, Sorbid SA, Sorbitrate, Suscard Buccal, Sustac, Synadrin, Transiderm-Nitro, Tridil, Tildiem*, Vascardin.

Generic names: diltiazem*, glyceryl trinitrate, isosorbide dinitrate, isosorbide mononitrate, lidoflazine, nifedipine*, pentaerythritol tetranitrate, perhexiline maleate, prenylamine, verapamil*.

Most of these drugs are unusually safe for occasional use. Unwanted effects include flushing, headache, dizziness and faintness. Longer-acting preparations may cause swollen ankles.

Drugs marked * are calcium antagonists. They may cause nausea, vomiting, constipation, and bradycardia (slow heartbeat). These are new drugs and their range of potential adverse effects is uncertain.

Lidoflazine (Clinium) and prenylamine (Synadrin) can precipitate heart-rate abnormalities, nausea, vomiting, diarrhoea, dizziness, noises in the ears and headaches. Sudden withdrawal may cause worsening angina.

Perhexiline maleate (Pexid) is the only drug in this group which has serious dangers. It is capable of causing nerve injury (peripheral neuropathy), raised pressure in the skull and liver damage. It must be withdrawn immediately if any of the following symptoms develop: pins and needles, staggering gait, muscle weakness, bleeding from the retina (you may notice persistent black shapes floating about in the visual field), visual impairment, low blood sugar, weight loss, jaundice and liver pain.

Peripheral Vasodilators

Brand names: Bradilan, Hexopal, Opilon, Paroven, Pernivit, Ronicol, Stugeron Forte, Vasculit.
Generic names: bamethan sulphate, cinnarizine, nicofuranose and nicotinic acid derivatives, oxpentifylline, thymoxamine.

Side-effects of these drugs include allergic reactions, rashes, flushing, dizziness, headache, nausea, palpitations and faintness.

Cerebral Vasodilators

Brand names: Cyclobral, Cyclospasmol, Defencin CP, Duvalidan, Hydergine, Praxilene.
Generic names: co-dergocrine mesylate, cyclandelate, isoxsuprine hydrochloride, naftidrofuryl oxalate.

Side-effects of these drugs are similar to peripheral vasodilators, above.

Anticoagulants

Brand names: Dindevan, Marevan, Sinthrome, Warfarin WBP.
Generic names: nicoumalone, phenindione, warfarin sodium.

Warfarin is the well-known rat poison. Too high a dose of anticoagulant will kill a person as effectively as a rat, by inducing internal bleeding. The hazard of these drugs even in normal dose is bleeding into the tissues.

Even aspirin, a weak anticoagulant, is capable of causing bleeding problems in mothers and babies. *Never* take an aspirin in the month before a baby is due – if possible, avoid aspirin throughout pregnancy.

Drugs which Reduce Blood Cholesterol

Brand names: Atromid S, Bezalip, Bradilan, Colestid, Lurselle, Questran.
Generic names: bezafibrate, cholestyramine, clofibrate, nico-furanose, nicotinic acid, probucol.

The main side-effects of clofibrate and bezafibrate are nausea, abdominal pain, itching, impotence and gall bladder disease. These drugs seem to accelerate aging, and consequently increase risk of death from a wide range of causes.

Cholestyramine (Questran) and colestipol (Colestid) bind bile salts in the gut. Side-effects include nausea, constipation or diarrhoea, heartburn, flatulence, rashes and reduced absorption of dietary vitamins.

Exercise

This is a brief list of activities to help you get started on the road to physical fitness and heart health. They start with a very gentle routine suitable for those who are under stress or unaccustomed to physical activity. If you are unfit or overweight, you should choose a gentle activity and do it every day.

As you grow fitter, your exercise routine can become more strenuous. Allow a day's recovery between sessions of vigorous activity – do something gentle like walking on alternate days. Do not allow your heart-rate to rise above the levels given on p. 231, below.

Dance

We want you to think about dance as one of the oldest forms of human recreation (re-creation). Dance has always fulfilled a variety of needs: self-expression, relaxation, transcendence, communication, and a number of other emotional needs. Our mundane world limits this advantageous activity mainly to the young. This is wrong. All ages need to regain the innate abilities of dance.

Do not believe you are: too old, too fat, too awkward or too ugly. None of that is important. You may be self-conscious, most of us are. But dance can turn and twist that into something more valuable: consciousness of self.

There are two routes to dance. One is to become totally conscious of every part of your body, to direct each movement and posture and timing; this is the method of the professional dancer. The other is to feel every part of your being; to evolve your movement as a partnership between the facets of your self, let your body influence its own direction with your mind as the means.

Take the feeling route. Try to let movement slide into you, using music as the stimulus. Movement should pervade and persuade you, take you along. Let go. Let it take you wherever it will! It may be a soft, sensuous experience or a driving physical expression of feeling.

Dance can regenerate the very core of your being. Because it is a self-directed activity, it will involve many levels of being, both physical and mental, in creating feedback loops. These can build up sensations and energy, becoming almost frighteningly exhilarating, or just a gentle exploration of part of your self. Either way, the ancient rhythms will help you unlock and grow.

How do you do it?

To begin with, you will start with simple conscious movements to suitable music, copying the way you've seen others move. Think of all the dance from cultures around the world: maybe you incline towards the African sometimes? Or is there a little of the stamping Aborigine about you? Don't let yourself be limited by our society's assumptions about dance.

You may find it easier if you watch yourself in a large mirror – but not if the mirror puts you off! You may want to introduce some of the jogging/jumping movements you do as exercise. Fine. While you are moving, try to relax enough to let your body take over. The music should help. Listen to it, let your body go.

Think carefully when you choose your dancing music. You should select something that speaks to you personally, that communicates directly with your being. It could be anything from a Beethoven quartet to the Rolling Stones; it could be punk or romantic, or even disco dancing music. The crucial thing is that it moves you, and you move with it.

Don't be disheartened if nothing magical happens. Enjoy the music and the movement, and sooner or later it will.

Dance as long and as often as you like, alone or in company. See if you can get your partner to join in sometimes. But remember, you are dancing for yourself.

Walking

This most natural and healthy of human activities has almost become a forgotten art. During the New York transit strike in 1980, bookshops were flooded with titles such as *Walking for Beginners*, *Walking – The Easy Way*, and so on. It can be seen as an indication of the way we slide too easily behind the steering wheel and into a loss of activity. Even in major cities, supposedly characterised by hustle and hurry, people slouch along at a lethargic pace.

In the absence of any other major physical activity, we should walk briskly (4 mph+, 6.5 km/h+) for at least half an hour each day. For many people this single simple change in lifestyle would produce a vast improvement in their health and well-being.

We would like you to aim for half an hour's walk a day. When you do it is not important; you might be able to walk to and from work, spend half your lunch-hour walking, or leave your car a couple of miles away and complete the journey on foot. Alternatively, make an event of it in the evening – re-explore your neighbourhood. Once a week, perhaps on Sunday, you should consider a long walk of three or four hours' duration: one that will really physically tire you. Go in all weathers, come home to a favourite meal and hot bath. Make it part of a session of physical enjoyment.

On walking technique: think of the exaggerated ram-rod swing and stamp of the regimental sergeant major. It is part of his job to look a little comical. By exaggerating the required movements, it is his aim that those he is instructing pick up something of the right idea.

You don't have to join up, just straighten up. Check your position against a wall: head up, shoulders back, ribs raised. When you step forward, reach and dig your heel in to pull you forward, and push yourself on with the ball of your foot before you swing your leg forward once more. Get the most out of each leg movement. If this is working properly, you will find you have to swing your arms in order to balance the pull and push of your legs. Breathe deep and easy.

Experiment with different lengths of stride. Most people should take longer strides on a brisk walk than they normally would, and you may have to make a conscious effort to change your habits to move further with each step. Imagine you're wearing seven-league boots and use every inch of your legs.

Keep your body loose, shoulders straight but relaxed – don't let them sag forward, where they'll inhibit your breathing. Try imagining you're suspended by a string attached to the crown of your head which keeps your spine extended, head high on a long neck. Experience the feeling of pride that a loping stride and an upright body can give you. How easy, how natural it is!

In a matter of weeks you will find yourself striding along on healthier legs (in better shape, too), and will be amazed at the lack of ability of those around you. When you get to this stage, it will be time to move on. But don't hurry your programme. Take your time, work with your body, aim for enjoyment.

Do wear flat, comfortable shoes (running shoes or good quality trainers are excellent, unless you're taking paths over rough, wet ground) and suitable clothes. Get a shoulder bag to carry your waterproof, scarf and gloves. It will be useful for maps and compass if you get the 'walking bug' and become really adventurous.

Do warm up before your strenuous walks.

Do vary your pace – a change might be as good as a rest – as you go. You will feel your muscles working through a full and growing range of movement.

Do go fast enough to sweat. It is good for you. It shows your systems are working properly, and refreshes the skin.

Do not put up with pain. Minor muscular aches that rests dispel can be ignored – but not persistent or sharp pain. It is a warning that some part of your body is overloaded. Ease up, go home, rest and recover. There will be other days. Maybe your systems were preoccupied with fighting off infection; take it a little easier next time, increase the pace later in your walk.

Above all, don't give up! Walking is the activity to continue with till you're past ninety.

More Strenuous Activities

Heart health is maximised by activities which develop stamina. Walking, running, dancing, swimming and cycling are ideal. Weight training can be excellent, if you go for repeated fast movements with light weights. Working out with the sort of heavy weights that are used to build bulging muscles is as likely to damage your heart as strengthen it.

The following activities build stamina. They are arranged in declining order of effectiveness. Pick the ones you enjoy and then try some of the others – you may find you enjoy learning them too.

Running	Squash
Jogging	Football
Swimming (hard)	Brisk walking
Cycling (hard)	Tennis
Hill walking	Gymnastics

Disco dancing

Canoeing

Stair climbing

Digging (garden)

Judo

Mowing lawn by hand

Badminton

Cardiovascular conditioning occurs when your heart is beating hard and you are breathing deeply. Do not try to keep your mouth shut, breathe through nose or mouth according to your oxygen need. Aim for a heart-rate that does not rise above the upper limit for your age given in the table below. If you have any difficulty finding your pulse at your wrist, try feeling just below the corner of your jaw for the pulse in your throat. Count the number of beats in 15 seconds.

	Desirable maximum pulse rate	
Age	*beats/minute*	*beats in 15 seconds*
20–29	140	35
30–39	132	33
40–49	122	31
50–59	114	28
60–69	106	26

Recommended Books

On the heart and heart disease:
Carruthers, M. *The Western Way of Death*. London: Davis Poynter, 1974.
Lynch, J. *The Broken Heart: The Medical Consequences of Loneliness*. New York: Basic Books, 1977.
McCormick, E. *The Heart Attack Recovery Book*. London: Coventure, 1984.
Nixon, P. 'Take heart'. In *The BMA Book of Executive Health*. London: Times Books, 1979.

On medicine and treatment:
Dubos, R. *The Mirage of Health*. London: Allen & Unwin, 1960.
Inglis, B. *The Diseases of Civilization*. London: Hodder & Stoughton, 1981.
Melville, A. and Johnson, C. *Cured to Death: The Effects of Prescription Drugs*. London: New English Library, 1983.

On drugs (reference):
Martindale: The Extra Pharmacopoeia. London: The Pharmaceutical Press, 1983.
Parish, P. *Medicines: A Guide for Everybody*. London: Penguin, 1983 (4th ed.).

On health and fitness:
Looking After Yourself: free pamphlet from the Health Education Council, 78 New Oxford Street, London W1A 1AH.
Pelletier, K. *Mind as Healer, Mind as Slayer*. New York: Dell, 1977.
Physical Fitness: 5BX 11-minute-a-day plan for men, XBX 12-minute-a-day plan for women. Exercises developed by the Royal Canadian Air Force. Harmondsworth: Penguin Books, 1964.
The Sunday Times New Book of Body Maintenance. London: Mermaid Books, 1982.
Well Being: Helping Yourself to Good Health. A Channel 4 book, based on the TV series presented by Pam Armstrong. Harmondsworth: Penguin, 1982.

On food and dealing with fat:
Cannon, G. and Einzig, H. *Dieting Makes You Fat*. London: Century, 1983.
Dufty, W. *Sugar Blues*. Tunbridge Wells: Abacus, 1980.
McCance, R. A. and Widdowson, E. M. *The Composition of Foods*. London: Her Majesty's Stationery Office, 1978.
Orbach, S. *Fat is a Feminist Issue*. London: Hamlyn, 1979.

On the environment:
Meadows, D., Meadows, D., Randers, J. and Behrens, W. *The Limits to Growth*. London: Pan Books, 1974.
Rural Resettlement Handbook. Prism Alpha in association with Lighthouse Books. 3rd ed., 1984.

Useful Organisations

ASH (Action on Smoking and Health), 5–11 Mortimer Street, London W1N 7RH, (01) 637 9843. Free information on giving up smoking, plus list of smoking withdrawal clinics.

British Association for Counselling, 37A Sheep Street, Rugby CV21 3BX, (0788) 78328/9. Gives information on counselling services.

Health Education Council, 78 New Oxford Street, London W1A 1AH, (01) 637 1881. Provides free information and leaflets on health topics. There is also a library which can be used by anyone, and helpful staff.

McCarrison Society, 23 Stanley Court, Worcester Road, Sutton, Surrey SM2 6SD. Provides advice on nutrition.

National Marriage Guidance Council, Herbert Gray College, Little Church Street, Rugby, Warwicks. CV21 3AP. Local branches can be found under Marriage Guidance in the telephone directory.

Overeaters Anonymous, c/o 182 Hutton Road, Brentwood, Essex CM15 8NS. Organisation designed to help people with eating problems.

Positive Health Centre, 15 Fitzroy Square, London W1P 5HQ, (01) 388 1007. Commercial organisation offering deep relaxation training and therapy.

The Psychotherapy Centre, 67 Upper Berkeley Street, London W1H 7TH, (01) 262 8852. Can refer psychotherapists.

Scottish Health Education Group, Woodburn House, Canaan Lane, Edinburgh EH10 4SG, (031) 447 8044.

Scottish Marriage Guidance Council, 58 Palmerston Place, Edinburgh EH12 5AZ, (031) 225 5006. Can give details of counselling services in Scotland.

Life Profile Limited is a health advisory service which uses a computer data base to generate individual health plans for subscribers. It is a dispersed organisation which can be contacted via 37B New Cavendish Street, London W1M 8JR.

References

Introduction/Chapter 1

Beral, V. 'Cardiovascular disease mortality trends and oral contraceptive use in young women.' *Lancet, 2,* 1976, 1047–52.

Boyer, J. L. and Wilmore, J. H. 'Physical Fitness Programs for Children.' In: Amsterdam, E. A. *et al* (eds.) *Exercise in Cardiovascular Health and Disease.* New York: Yorke Medical Books, 1977.

British Heart Foundation, *Heart Bulletin,* 1984.

Campbell, M. J. *et al* 'Chest pain in women: a study of prevalence and mortality follow up in South Wales.' *Journal of Epidemiology and Community Health, 38,* 1984, 17–20.

Fry, J. 'Coronary Artery Diseases.' *Update,* 1 July 1979, 62–65.

Howe, G. M. *et al* 'Cardiovascular disease.' In: Howe, M. G. (ed.) *A World Geography of Human Diseases.* London: Academic Press, 1977.

Nixon, P. G. F. 'Are there clinically significant prodromal signs and symptoms of impending sudden death?' *Practical Cardiology, 8,* 1982, 175–183.

Ovcarov, V. K. and Bystrova, V. A. 'Present trends in mortality in the age group 35–64 in selected developed countries between 1950–1973.' *World Health Statistics Report, 31,* 1978, 308–346.

Preston, *Mortality Patterns in National Populations.* London: Academic Press, 1976.

Puska, P. *et al* 'Changes in coronary risk factors during comprehensive five-year community programme to control cardiovascular diseases (North Karelia project).' *British Medical Journal, 2,* 1979, 1173–1178.

Smith, W. C. *et al* letter, *British Medical Journal, 289,* ii, 1984, 1455.

Trowell, H. and Burkitt, D. (eds.) *Western Diseases: their emergence and prevention.* London: Edward Arnold, 1981.

Chapters 2 and 3

Baroldi, G. *et al* 'Degree of coronary artery obstruction at autopsy in patients with coronary heart disease compared with "control" population.' In: A. Maseri (ed.) *Primary and Secondary Angina Pectoris.* Grune & Stratton, 1977.

Chave, S. P. W. *et al* 'Vigorous exercise in leisure time and death rate: a study of male civil servants.' *Journal of Epidemiology and Community Health, 32,* 1978, 239–243.

Dawber, T. R. *The Framingham Study.* Boston: Harvard University Press, 1980.

Gorridge, J. A. L. 'A fresh look at what everybody knows about ischaemic heart disease': discussion paper. *Journal of the Royal Society of Medicine, 77,* 1984, 390–398.

Heller, R. F. *et al* 'How well can we predict coronary heart disease? Findings in the United Kingdom Heart Disease Prevention Project.' *British Medical Journal, 288,* 1984, 1409–11.

Lapidus, L. *et al* 'Distribution of adipose tissue and risk of cardiovascular disease and death: a 12 year follow up of participants in the population study of women in Gothenburg, Sweden.' *British Medical Journal, 289,* 1984, 1257–1261.

Larsson, B. *et al* 'Abdominal adipose tissue distribution, obesity, and risk of cardiovascular disease and death: 13 year follow up of participants in the study of men born in 1913.' *British Medical Journal, 288,* 1984, 1401–1404.

McDonald, C. *et al* (eds.) *Very early detection of coronary heart disease.* Oxford: Exerpta Medica, 1978.

MacGregor, G. A. 'Dietary sodium and potassium and blood pressure.' *Lancet,* 2 April 1983, 750–2.

Magarian, G. J. 'Hyperventilation syndromes: infrequently recognised common expressions of anxiety and stress.' *Medicine, 61, 4,* 1982, 219–236.

Mann, G. V. 'Diet-Heart: end of an era.' *New England Journal of Medicine, 297,* 1977, 644–650.

Rauramaa, R. *et al* 'Effects of mild physical exercise on serum lipoproteins and metabolites of arachidonic acid: a controlled randomised trial in middle aged men.' *British Medical Journal, 288,* 1984, 603.

Rose, G. 'Incubation period of coronary heart disease.' *British Medical Journal, 284,* 1982, 1600–1.

'Royal College of General Practitioners' Oral Contraception Study: Incidence of arterial disease among oral contraceptive users.' *Journal of the Royal College of General Practitioners, 33,* 1983, 75–82.

Shekelle, R. B. *et al* 'Diet, serum cholesterol, and death from coronary heart disease.' *New England Journal of Medicine, 304, 2,* 1981, 65–70.

Shephard, R. J. *Ischaemic Heart Disease and Exercise.* London: Croom Helm, 1981.

Slone, D. *et al* 'Risk of myocardial infarction in relation to current and discontinued use of oral contraceptives.' *New England Journal of Medicine, 305, 8,* 1980, 420–424.

Stadel, B. V. 'Oral contraceptives and cardiovascular disease.' *New England Journal of Medicine, 305,* 1981, 672–7.

World Health Organisation. *Prevention of Coronary Heart Disease: Report of a WHO Expert Committee.* Technical Report Series 678, WHO, Geneva, 1982.

Yudkin, J. *Pure, White, and Deadly.* London: Davis-Poynter, 1972.

Yudkin, J. *et al* 'Effects of high dietary sugar.' *British Medical Journal, 281,* 1980, 1396.

Chapter 4

British Medical Association and The Pharmaceutical Society of Great Britain, *British National Formulary,* Number 8, 1984.

Burr, M. L. *et al* 'Need for maintenance diuretic treatment.' *British Medical Journal,* 1977, 976–7.

Consumers Association: 'The Calcium Antagonists: an important new group of drugs.' *Drug and Therapeutics Bulletin, 22, 17*, August 1984.

Department of Health and Social Security, *Health and Personal Social Services Statistics*. London: HMSO, 1983.

Dunkman, W. B. *et al* 'Medical perspectives in coronary artery surgery – a caveat.' *Annals of Internal Medicine, 81*, 1974, 817–837.

Frick, M. H. *et al* 'Influence of coronary bypass surgery on sudden death in chronic artery disease.' In: V. Manninen (ed.) *Sudden Coronary Death*. Basel: Karger, 1978.

Griggs, B. *Green Pharmacy*. London: Jill Norman & Hobhouse, 1981.

Hampton, J.R. 'Coronary artery bypass grafting for the reduction of mortality: an analysis of the trials.' *British Medical Journal, 289*, 1984, 1166–1170.

Inglis, B. *The Diseases of Civilization*. London: Hodder & Stoughton, 1981.

Kaplan, N. M. 'Whom to treat: the dilemma of mild hypertension.' *American Heart Journal*, 1981, 867–70.

Lewis, J. G. 'Adverse effects of oral diuretics.' *Adverse Drug Reaction Bulletin, 109*, 1984, 404–407.

Melville, A. and Johnson, C. *Cured to Death: the effects of prescription drugs*. London: Secker & Warburg, 1982.

Nixon, P. G. F. 'The responsibility of the cardiological mapmaker.' Editorial: *American Heart Journal, 100, 2*, 1980, 139–143.

Office of Health Economics, *Health Statistics*. London: OHE, 1984.

Chapters 5 and 6

Brenner, H. 'Economic Policy: Implications for mental and physical health and criminal aggression.' *Joint Econ. Comm. Congress No. 5*, US Government Printing Office, 1976.

Brenner, H. 'The importance of the economy to a nation's health: the case of post war England and Wales.' Paper given at a conference on Unemployment and Health, Welsh National School of Medicine, Cardiff, 10 April 1981.

Carruthers, M. *The Western Way of Death*. London: Davis-Poynter, 1974.

Cochrane, A. L. '1931–71: a critical review with particular reference to the medical profession.' In: Medicines for the Year 2000, Office of Health Economics, London, 1979.

Friedman, M. and Rosenman, R. *Type A Behaviour and Your Heart*. London: Wildwood House, 1974.

Lynch, J. J. *The Broken Heart: the medical consequences of loneliness*. New York: Basic Books, 1977.

Najman, J. M. and Congleton, A. 'Australian occupational mortality, 1965–7: cause specific or general susceptibility?' *Sociology of Health and Illness, 1*, 1979, 158–76.

Nixon, P. G. F. 'Stress, life-style, and cardiovascular disease: a cardiological odyssey.' A paper presented at the inaugural conference of the British Holistic Medical Association, 24/25 September, 1983.

Sterling, P. and Eyer, J. 'Biological basis of stress-related mortality.' *Social Science and Medicine, 13E*, 1981, 3–42.

Chapter 7
Leakey, R. and Lewin, R. *People of the Lake*. London: Pelican, 1981.
Meadows, D. *et al The Limits to Growth*. London: Pan, 1974.
Sheldrake, R. *A New Science of Life*. London: Paladin, 1983.

Chapter 8
Amsterdam, E. A. *et al* 'Exercise training in coronary heart disease: is there a cardiac effect?' Also: 'Control and modulation of stress emotions.' In: Amsterdam, E. A. *et al* (eds.) *Exercise in Cardiovascular Health and Disease*. New York: Yorke Medical Books, 1977.
Hellstrom, H.R. 'Coronary artery vasospasm: the likely immediate cause of acute myocardial infarction.' *British Heart Journal, 41*, 1979, 426–432.
Nixon, P. G. F. 'Effort and the heart.' 'Opinions', Channel 4 TV, 6th August 1984.
Nixon, P. G. F. 'Stress and the cardiovascular system.' *The Practitioner, 226*, 1982, 1589–1598.
Nixon, P. G. F. *et al Arrhythmic hyperventilation in cardiac rehabilitation*. Unpublished manuscript.
Nixon, P. G. F. and Bethell, H. J. N. 'Preinfarction ill health.' (Editorial), *The American Journal of Cardiology, 33*, 1974, 446–9.
Wilcox, R. G. *et al* 'Is exercise good for high blood pressure?' *British Medical Journal, 285*, 1982, 767–9.

Chapter 9
Paul, A. A. and Southgate, D. A. T.: McCance and Widdowson's *The Composition of Foods*. (4th ed.) London: HMSO, 1978.

Index